Opening Shots: 1914

Opening Shots: 1914

Personal Accounts by Allied Soldiers & Sailors
From the First Battles of the Great War

In the Firing Line
A. St. John Adcock

With My Regiment
"Platoon Commander"
(Arthur Mills)

LEONAUR

Opening Shots: 1914
Personal Accounts by Allied Soldiers & Sailors
From the First Battles of the Great War
In the Firing Line
by A. St. John Adcock
and
With My Regiment
by "Platoon Commander" (Arthur Mills)

First published under the titles
In the Firing Line
and
With My Regiment

FIRST EDITION

Leonaur is an imprint
of Oakpast Ltd

ISBN: 978-1-78282-221-9 (hardcover)
ISBN: 978-1-78282-222-6(softcover)

http://www.leonaur.com

Contents

In the Firing Line

CHARGE OF BRITISH HUSSARS AGAINST GERMAN CUIRASSIERS
IN A VILLAGE OF NORTHERN FRANCE

Contents

1

Introduction: The Baptism of Fire

(Written by the author:1914)

"E'en now their vanguard gathers,
E'en now we face the fray."
Kipling.—*Hymn before Action,*

The war correspondent has become old-fashioned before he has had time to grow old; he was made by telegraphy, and wireless has unmade him. The swift transmission of news from the front might gratify us who are waiting anxiously at home, but such news can be caught in the air now, or secretly and as swiftly retransmitted so as to gratify our enemies even more by keeping them well-informed of our strength and intentions and putting them on their guard. Therefore our armies have rightly gone forth on this the greatest war the world has ever seen as they went to the Crusades, with no Press reporter in their ranks, and when the historian sits down, some peaceful day in the future, to write his prose epic of the Titanic struggle that is now raging over Europe he will have no records of the actual fighting except such as he can gather from the necessarily terse official reports, the published stories of refugees and wounded soldiers that have been picked up by enterprising newspaper men hovering alertly in the rear of the forces, and from the private letters written to their friends by the fighting men themselves.

These letters compensate largely for the ampler, more expert accounts the war correspondent is not allowed to send us. They may tell little of strategic movements or of the full tide and progress of an engagement till you read them in conjunction with the official reports, but in their vivid, spontaneous revelations of what the man in battle has seen and felt, in the intensity of their human interest they have a unique value beyond anything to be found in more professional military or journalistic documents. They so unconsciously express the personality and spirit of their writers; the very homeliness of their language adds wonderfully and unintentionally to their effectiveness; there is rarely any note of boastfulness even in a moment of triumph; they record the most splendid heroisms casually, sometimes even flippantly, as if it were merely natural to see such things happening about them, or to be doing such things themselves. If they tell of hardships it is to laugh at them; again and again there are little bursts of affection and admiration for their officers and comrades—they are the most potent of recruiting literature, these letters, for a mere reading of them thrills the stay-at-home with pride that these good fellows are his countrymen and with a sort of angry shame that his age or his safe civilian responsibilities keep him from being out there taking his stand beside them.

The courage, the cheerfulness, the dauntless spirit of them is the more striking when you remember that the vast majority of our soldiers have never been in battle until now. Russia has many veterans from her war with Japan; France has a few who fought the Prussian enemy in 1870; we have some from the Boer war; but fully three parts of our troops, like all the heroic Belgians, have had their baptism of fire in the present gigantic conflict. And it is curiously interesting to read in several of the letters the frank confession of their writers' feelings when they came face to face for the first time with the menace of death in action. One such note, published in various papers, was from Alfred Bishop, a sailor who took part in the famous North Sea engagement of August last. His ship's mascot is a black cat, and:

> Our dear little black kitten sat under our foremost gun during the whole battle, and was not frightened at all, only when we first started firing. But afterwards she sat and licked herself. . . . Before we started fighting we were all very nervous, but after we joined in we were all happy and most of us laughing till it was finished. Then we all sobbed and cried. Even if I never come back don't think I died a painful death. Everything yesterday was quick as lightning.

A wounded English gunner telling of how he went into action near Mons owns to the same touch of nervousness in the first few minutes:

> What does it feel like to be under fire? Well, the first shot makes

you a bit shaky. It's a surprise packet. You have to wait and keep on moving till you get a chance.

But as soon as the chance came, his shakiness went, and his one desire in hospital was:

To get back to the front as soon as the doctor says I'm fit to man a gun. I don't want to stop here.

A young Frenchman at the front writes to his parents:

I have received my baptism of fire in Paris. I heard the bullets whistling at my ears, and saw my poor comrades fall around me. The first minutes are dreadful. They are the worst. You feel wild. You hesitate; you don't know what to do. Then, after a time, you feel quite at your ease in this atmosphere of lead.

A wounded Frenchman writes to a friend in London:

I am in the field hospital now, with a nice little hole in my left shoulder, through which a bullet of one of the War Lord's military subjects has passed. My shoulder feels much as if some playful joker has touched it with a lighted cigar. . . . It is strange, but in the face of death and destruction I catch myself trying to make out where the shell has fallen, as if I were an interested spectator at a rifle competition. And I was not the only one. I saw many curious faces around me, bearing expressions full of interest, just as if the owners of the respective faces formed the auditorium of a highly fascinating theatrical performance, without having anything to do with the play itself.
The impression crossed my mind in one-thousandth part of a second, and was followed by numerous others, altogether alien from the most serious things which were happening and going to happen. The human mind is a curious and complicated thing. Now that we were shooting at the enemy, and often afterwards in the midst of a fierce battle, I heard some remark made or some funny expression used which proved that the speaker's thoughts were far from realising the terrible facts around him. It has nothing to do with heartlessness or anything like that. I don't know yet what it is. Perhaps I shall have an opportunity to philosophise on it later on.

There is a curious comment in a letter from Sergeant Major Mac-Dermott, who writes during the great retreat from Mons, when everybody had become inured to the atmosphere of the battlefield.

We're wonderfully cheerful, and happy as barelegged urchins scampering over the fields.

It is the quantity not the quality of the German shells that are having effect on us, and it's not so much the actual damage to life as the hellish nerve-racking noise that counts for so much. Townsmen who are used to the noise of the streets can stand it a lot better than the countrymen, and I think you will find that by far the fittest are those regiments recruited in the big cities. A London lad near me says it is no worse than the roar of motor-buses in the City on a busy day."

But the most graphic and minutely detailed picture of the psychic experiences of a soldier plunged for the first time into the pandemonium of a modern battle is given in the *Retch* by a wounded Russian artillery officer writing from a St. Petersburg hospital.

I cannot say where we fought, for we are forbidden to divulge that, but I will tell you my own experiences. In times of peace one has no conception of what a battle really means. When war was declared our brigade was despatched to the theatre of operations. I went with delight, and so did the others. When we reached our destination we were told that the battle would begin in the morning.

At daybreak positions were assigned to us, and the commander of the brigade handed us a plan of the action of our artillery. From that moment horror possessed our souls. It was not anxiety for ourselves or fear of the enemy, but a feeling of awe in the face of something unknown. At six o'clock we opened fire at a mark which we could not distinguish, but which we understood to be the enemy.

Towards midday we were informed that the German cavalry was attempting to envelop our right wing, and were ordered in that direction. Having occupied our new position we waited. Suddenly we see the enemy coming, and at the same time he opens fire on us. We turn our guns upon him, and I give the order to fire. I myself feel that I am in a kind of nightmare. Our battery officers begin to melt away. I see that the Germans are developing their attack. First one regiment appears, and then another. I direct the guns and pour a volley of projectiles right into the thick of the first regiment. Then a second volley, and a third. I see how they fall among the men, and can even discern the severed limbs of the dead flying into the air after the explosion.

One of the enemy's regiments is annihilated. Then a second one. All this time I am pouring missiles in among them. But now the nervous feeling has left me. My soul is filled with hate, and I continue to shoot at the enemy without the least feeling of pity.

Yet still the enemy is advancing, rushing forward and lying down in turns. I do not understand his tactics, but what are they to me? It is enough for me that I am occupying a favourable position and mowing him down like a strong man with a scythe in a clover field.

During the first night after the battle I could not sleep a wink. All the time my mind was filled with pictures of the battlefield. I saw German regiments approaching, and myself firing right into the thick of them. Heads, arms, legs, and whole bodies of men were being flung high into the air. It was a dreadful vision.

I was in four battles. When the second began I went into it like an automaton. Only your muscles are taxed. All the rest of your being seems paralyzed. So complete is the suspension of the sensory processes that I never felt my wound. All I remember is that a feeling of giddiness came over me, and my head began to swim. Then I swooned to the ground, and was picked up by the Medical Corps and carried to the rear.

2

The Four Days' Battle Near Mons

"And turning to his men,
Quoth our brave Henry then,
'Though they be one to ten,
Be not amazed.'"
    Michael Drayton.

Most of us are old enough, (as at time of first publication), to remember how, when we entered upon the South African Campaign—Boer War—(as when we started the Crimean and other of our wars) the nation was divided against itself; passionate, bitter controversies were waged between anti-Boer and pro-Boer—between those who considered the war an unjust and those who considered it a just one. This time there has been nothing of that. Sir Edward Grey's resolute efforts for peace proving futile, as soon as Germany tore up her obligations of honour, that "scrap of paper," and began to pour her huge, boastedly irresistible armies into Belgium, we took up the gauge she so insolently flung to us, and the one feeling from end to end of the Empire was of devout thankfulness that our government had so instantly done the only right and honourable thing; all political parties, all classes flung their differences behind them unhesitatingly and stood four-square at once against the common enemy. They were heartened by a sense of relief, even, that the swaggering German peril which had been darkly menacing us for years had materialised and was upon us at last, that we were coming to grips with it and should have the chance of ending it once and for ever.

But immediately after our declaration of war on August 4th, a strange secrecy and silence fell like an impenetrable mask over all our military movements. In our cities and towns we were troubled with business disorganisations, but that mystery, that waiting in suspense, troubled us far more. News came that the fighting continued furiously on the Belgian frontier; that it was beginning on the fringes of Alsace; that the Russians were advancing victoriously on East Prussia; and still though our own army was mobilised and we were eagerly starting to raise a new and a larger one, we rightly learned no more, perhaps less, than the enemy could of what our Expeditionary Force was doing or where it was.

Last time we were at war we had seen regiment after regiment go off with bands playing and with cheering multitudes lining the roads as they passed; this time we had no glimpse of their going; did not know when they went, or so much as whether they were gone. One day rumour landed them safely in France or Belgium; the next it assured us that they were not yet ready to embark; and the next it had rushed them, as by magic, right across Belgium and credited them with standing shoulder to shoulder in the fighting line with the magnificent defenders of Liege.

But the glory of that defence, as we were soon to find out, belongs to Belgium alone; the Germans had hacked their way through and were nearing Mons before our men were able to get far enough north to come in touch with them. Not that they had lost any time on the road. It took a fortnight to mobilise and equip them; they sailed from Southampton on August 17th, and four days later were at Mons and under fire. This much and more you may gather from a diary-letter that was published in the *Western Daily Press:*

Letter 1.—From Sapper George Bryant, Royal Engineers, to his father, Mr. J. J. Bryant, of Fishponds:

Aug. 17.—Sailed from Southampton, on *Manchester Engineer,* 4.45 a.m.

Aug. 18.—Landed Rouen, 6.20 a.m. Proceeded to rest camp at the Racecourse, Rouen.

Aug. 19.—Left camp 9 p.m., and entrained to Aulnoye.

Aug. 20.—Marched to Fiezines.

Aug. 21.—Marched to Mons, and proceeded to the canal, to obstacle the bridges and prepare for blowing up. Barricaded the main streets. Saw German cavalry, and was under fire.

Aug. 22.—Severe fighting and terrible. Went to blow up bridges with Lieut. Day, who was shot at my side through the nose. Unable to destroy bridges owing to such heavy firing of the Germans. Sight heart-breaking. Women and children driven from their homes by point of bayonet, and marched through streets in front of Germans, who fired behind them and through their armpits. Therefore, our fellows were unable to fire back. They rolled up in thousands, about 100 to our one. Went from here to dig trenches for infantry retreating. Was soon under fire, and had to retreat, and infantry took our position, and were completely wiped out (Middlesex).

Aug. 23.—Severe fighting and bombarding of a town, shells bursting around us. Retreated, and dug trenches for infantry, but soon had fire about us, and retreated again and marched to take up position for next day, which was to be a rest, us having had but very little.

Aug. 24.—Were unable to rest. Germans pressed us hotly, and fired continually. One of their aeroplanes followed our route, and was fired at. One of our lieutenants chased it, and eventually succeeded in shooting the aviator through the head, and he came to earth. Three aeroplanes were captured this day. We had no close fighting, and marched away to take up a position for next day's fighting, which was a hard day's work.

Aug. 25.—We tried to destroy an orchard, but drew the Germans' artillery fire, which was hot and bursting around us. We continued our work until almost too late, and had to retire to infantry lines, and had it hot in doing so. I was stood next to General Shaw's aide-camp who was badly wounded, but was not touched myself. We dug trenches for infantry, and then marched to join the 2nd Division, but fire was too hot to enable us to do our work. Germans were surrounded by us to the letter " C," and we were waiting for the French to come up on our right flank, but they did not arrive. On returning from the 2nd Division two shells, one after another, burst in front of us, first destroying a house; the second, I received my wound in left leg, being the only fellow hit out of 180. Was placed on tool cart, and taken to Field Hospital, but rest there was short, owing to Germans firing on hospital. Orderlies ran off and left us three to take our chance. Germans blew up church and hospital in same village, and were firing on ours when I was helped out

18

by the other two fellows, and on to a cart, which overtook the ambulance, which I was put on, and travelled all night to St. Quentin and was entrained there at 9.30 a.m. Aug. 26.

Aug. 26.—Travelled all day, reaching Rouen, Aug. 27, and was taken to Field Hospital on Racecourse.

We shall have to wait some time yet for full and coherent accounts of the fierce fighting at Mons, but from the soldiers' letters and the stories of the wounded one gets illuminating glimpses of that terrific four-days' battle.

Letter 2.—From Driver W. Moore, Royal Field Artillery, to the superintendent of the *Cornwall* training ship, of which Driver Moore is an "old boy "still under twenty:

It was Sunday night when we saw the enemy. We were ready for action, but were lying down to have a rest, when orders came to stand at our posts. It was about four a.m. on Monday when we started to fire; we were at it all day till six p.m., when we started to advance. Then the bugle sounded the charge, and the cavalry and infantry charged like madmen at the enemy; then the enemy fell back about forty miles, so we held them at bay till Wednesday, when the enemy was reinforced. Then they came on to Mons, and by that time we had every man, woman, and child out of the town.

We were situated on a hill in a cornfield and could see all over the country. It was about three p.m., and we started to let them have a welcome by blowing up two of their batteries in about five minutes; then the infantry let go, and then the battle was in full swing.

In the middle of the battle a driver got wounded and asked to see the colours before he died, and he was told by an officer that the guns were his colours. He replied, "Tell the drivers to keep their eyes on their guns, because if we lose our guns we lose our colours."

Just then the infantry had to retire, and the gunners had to leave their guns, but the drivers were so proud of their guns that they went and got them out, and we retired to St. Quentin. We had a roll-call, and only ten were left out of my battery. This was the battle in which poor Winchester (another old *Cornwall* boy) lost his life in trying to get the guns away.

Letter 3.—From Private G. Moody, to his parents at Beckenham:

I was at Mons in the trenches in the firing-line for twenty-four hours, and my regiment was ordered to help the French on the right. Poor old A Company was left to occupy the trenches and to hold them: whatever might happen, they were not to leave them. There were about 250 of us, and the Germans came on, and as fast as we knocked them over more took their places. Well, out of 250 men only eighty were left, and we had to surrender. They took away everything, and we were lined up to be shot, so as to be no trouble to them. Then the cavalry of the French made a charge, and the Germans were cut down like grass. We got away, and wandered about all night, never knowing if we were walking into our chaps or the Germans. After walking about some time we commenced falling down through drinking water that had been poisoned, and then we were put into some motor-wagons and taken to Amiens.

Letter 4.—From a Lincolnshire sergeant to his brother:

It came unexpectedly. The first inkling we had was just after reveille, when our cavalry pickets fell back and reported the presence of the enemy in strength on our front and slightly to the left. In a few minutes we were all at our posts without the slightest confusion, and as we lay down in the trenches our artillery opened fire. It was a fine sight to see the shells speeding through the air to pay our respects to Kaiser Bill and his men. Soon the Germans returned the compliment; but they were a long time in finding anything approaching the range, and they didn't know of shelters—a trick we learned from the Boers, I believe. After about half an hour of this work their infantry came into view along our front. They were in solid square blocks standing out sharply against the skyline, and we couldn't help hitting them.

We lay in our trenches with not a sound or sign to tell them of what was before them. They crept nearer and nearer, and then our officers gave the word. Under the storm of bullets they seemed to stagger like drunken men, after which they made a run for us shouting some outlandish cry that we could not make out. Half way across the open another volley tore through their ranks, and by this time our artillery began dropping shells around them. Then an officer gave an order, and they broke into open formation, rushing like mad things towards the trenches on our left. Some of our men continued the volley firing, but a few of the crack shots were told off to indulge in independent firing for the benefit of the Germans. That is another trick taught us by Brother Boer, and our Germans did not like it at all. They fell back in confusion and then lay down wherever cover was available.

Letter 5.—From Private Levy, Royal Munster Fusiliers:

We were sent up to the firing line to try and save a battery. When we got there we found that they were nearly all killed or wounded. Our Irish lads opened fire on the dirty Germans, and you should have seen them fall. It was like a game of skittles. But as soon as you knocked them down up came another thousand or so. We could not make out where they came from. So, all of a sudden, our officers gave us the order to charge. We fixed bayonets and went like fire through them. You should have seen them run!

We had two companies of ours there against about 3,000 of theirs, and I tell you it was warm. I was not sorry when nighttime came, but that was not all. You see, we had no horses to get those guns away, and our chaps would not leave them.

We dragged them ourselves to a place of safety. As the firing line was at full swing we had with us an officer of the Hussars. I think he was next to me, and he had his hand nearly blown off by one of the German shells. So I and two more fellows picked him up and took him to a place of safety, where he got his wound cared for. I heard afterwards that he had been sent home, poor fellow.

Letter 6.—From Sergeant A. J. Smith, 1st Lincolnshire Regiment:

We smashed up the *Kaiser's* famous regiment—the Imperial Guards—and incidentally they gave us a shaking. They caught me napping. I got wounded on Sunday night, but I stuck it until Thursday. I could then go no further, so they put me in the ambulance and sent me home. It was just as safe in the firing line as in the improvised hospital, as when our force moved the Germans closed up and shelled the hospitals and burned the villages to the ground.

We started on Sunday, and were fighting and marching until

Thursday. Troops were falling asleep on the roadside until the shells started dropping, then we were very much awake.

I feel proud to belong to the British Army for the way in which they bore themselves in front of the other nations. No greater tribute could be paid us than what a German officer, who was captured, said. He said it was inferno to stand up against the British Army.

Letter 7.—From Private J. R. Tait, of the 2nd Essex Regiment:

We were near Mons when we had the order to entrench. It was just dawn when we were halfway down our trenches, and we were on our knees when the Germans opened a murderous fire with their guns and machine guns. We opened a rapid fire with our Maxims and rifles; we let them have it properly, but no sooner did we have one lot down than up came another lot, and they sent their cavalry to charge us, but we were there with our bayonets, and we emptied our magazines on them. Their men and horses were in a confused heap. There were a lot of wounded horses we had to shoot to end their misery.

We had several charges with their infantry, too. We find they don't like the bayonets. Their rifle shooting is rotten; I don't believe they could hit a haystack at 100 yards. We find their field artillery very good; we don't like their shrapnel; but I noticed that some did not burst; if one shell that came over me had burst I should have been blown to atoms; I thanked the Lord it did not. I also heard our men singing that famous song: "Get out and get under." I know that for an hour in our trench it would make anyone keep under, what with their shells and machine guns. Many poor fellows went to their death like heroes.

Letter 8.—From an Oldham private to his wife at Waterhead:

We have had a terrible time, and were in action for three days and nights. On Wednesday the officers said that Spion Kop was heaven to the fighting we had on that day. It is God help our poor fellows who get wounded in the legs or body and could not get off the battlefield, as when we retired the curs advanced and shot and bayoneted them as they tried to crawl away. They are rotten shots with the rifles. If they stood on Blackpool sands I don't believe they could hit the sea, but they are very good with the shrapnel guns, and nearly all our wounded have been hit with shrapnel bullets. Each shrapnel shell contains about 200 bullets which scatter all around, so just think what damage one shell can do when it drops among a troop of soldiers.

On the Tuesday our regiment went to the top of a hill which had a big flat top. An outpost of a Scotch regiment reported to us on our way up that all was clear, and we thought the enemy were about five miles away. We formed up in close formation—about 1,200 strong. Our commanding officer told us to pull our packs off, and start entrenching, but this was the last order he will ever give, for the enemy opened fire at us with five Maxim guns from a wood only 400 yards in front of us. They mowed us down like straw, and we could get no cover at all. Those who were left had to roll off the hill into the roadway—a long straight road—but we got it worse there. They had two shrapnel guns at the top of the road, and they did fearful execution to us and the Lancashire Fusiliers, who were also in the roadway. Any man who got out of that hell-hole should shake hands with himself.

This all happened before six o'clock in the morning. I have only seen about sixty of our regiment since. Our Maxim gun officer tried to fix his gun up during their murderous fire, but he got half his face blown away. We retired in splendid order about 300 yards, and then lined a ridge. Up to then we hardly fired a shot. They had nearly wiped three regiments out up to then, but our turn came. We gave them lead as fast as we could pull the triggers, and I think we put three Germans out to every one of our men accounted for. Bear in mind, they were about 250,000 strong to our 50,000. We got three Germans, and they said their officers told them that we were Russians and that England had not sent any men to fight.

They made us retire about five miles, and then we got the master of them, because our guns came up and covered the ground with dead Germans. The German gunners are good shots, but ours are a lot better. After we had shelled them a bit we got them on the run, and we drove them back to three miles behind where the battle started. We did give it them. I will say this, none of our soldiers touched any wounded Germans, though it took us all our time to keep our bayonets out of their ribs after seeing what they did with our wounded. But, thank God, we governed our tempers and left them alone.

I said we got the Germans on the run. And they can run! I picked up a few trophies and put them in my pack, but I got it blown off my back almost, so I had to discard it. I got one in the ribs, and then a horse got shot and fell on top of me, putting my shoulder out again and crushing my ribs. Otherwise I am fit to tackle a few more Germans, and I hope I shall soon be back again at the front to get a bit of my own back.

Letter 9.—From a private of the 1st Lincolns to friends at Barton-on-Humber:

Just a line to tell you I have returned from the front, and I can tell you we have had a very trying time of it. I must also say I am very lucky to be here. We were fighting from Sunday, 23rd, to Wednesday evening, on nothing to eat or drink—only the drop of water in our bottles which we carried. No one knows— only those that have seen us could credit such a sight, and if I live for years may I never see such a sight again. I can tell you it is not very nice to see your chum next to you with half his head blown off. The horrible sights I shall never forget. There seemed nothing else only certain death staring us in the face all the time. I cannot tell you all on paper. We must, however, look on the bright side, for it is no good doing any other. There are thousands of these Germans and they simply throw themselves at us. It is no joke fighting seven or eight to one. I can tell you we have lessened them a little, but there are millions more yet to finish.

Letter 10.— From one of the 9th Lancers to friends at Alfreton:

I was at the great Battle of Mons, and got a few shots in me. Once I was holding my officer's horse and my own, when, all of a sudden, a German shell came over and burst. Both horses were killed. I got away with my left hand split and three fingers blown in pieces. I am recovering rather quickly. I shall probably have to lose one or two of my fingers. I had two bullets taken from my body on Tuesday, and I can tell you I am in pain. I think I am one of the luckiest men in the world to escape as I did. War is a terrible thing. It is a lot different to what most of us expected.

Women and children leaving their homes with their belongings—then all of a sudden their houses would be in ashes,

THE BRITISH EXPEDITIONARY FORCE LANDS IN FRANCE,
AUGUST, 1914.

blown to the ground. I shall be glad to get well again. Then I can go and help again to fight the brutal Germans. The people in France and Belgium were so kind and good to our soldiers. They gave everything they possibly could do.

I have not heard from Jack (his brother, also at the front). I do so hope he will come back.

Letter 11.—From a wounded Gordon Highlander to his father, Mr. Alexander Buchan, of Monymusk:

We had a pretty stiff day of it last Sunday. The battalion went into small trenches in front of a wood a few miles to the right of Mons, and the Germans had the range to a yard. I was on the right edge of the wood with the machine guns, and there wasn't half some joy.

The shells were bursting all over the place. It was a bit of a funny sensation for a start, but you soon got used to it. You would hear it coming singing through the air over your head; then it would give a mighty big bang and you would see a great flash, and there would be a shower of lumps of iron and rusty nails all around your ears. They kept on doing that all Sunday; sometimes three or four at the same time, but none of them hit me. I was too fly for them.

Their artillery is pretty good, but the infantry are no good at all. They advance in close column, and you simply can't help hitting them. I opened fire on them with the machine gun and you could see them go over in heaps, but it didn't make any difference. For every man that fell ten took his place. That is their strong point. They have an unlimited supply of men.

They think they can beat any army in the world simply by hurling great masses of troops against them, but they are finding out their mistake now that they are put up against British troops.

The reason for the British retreat is this—all up through France are great lines of entrenchments and fortresses, and as they have not enough men to defeat the Germans in open battle, they are simply retiring from position to position—holding the Germans for a few days and then retiring to the next one. All this is just to gain time. Our losses are pretty severe, but they are nothing to the Germans, whose losses are ten to every one of ours.

Letter 12.—From Private J. Willis, of the Gordon Highlanders;

You mustn't run away with the notion that we stand shivering or cowering under shell fire, for we don't. We just go about our business in the usual way. If it's potting at the Germans that is to the fore we keep at it as though nothing were happening, and if we're just having a wee bit chat among ourselves we keep at it all the same.

Last week when I got this wound in my leg it was because I got excited in an argument with wee Georgie Ferriss, of our company, about Queen's Park Rangers and their chances this season. One of my chums was hit when he stood up to light a cigarette while the Germans were blazing away at us.

Keep your eyes wide open and you will have a big surprise sooner than you think. We're all right, and the Germans will find that out sooner than you at home.

Letter 13.—From Private G. Kay, of the 2nd Royal Scots, to his employer, a milkman, at Richmond:

You will be surprised to hear I am home from Belgium in hospital with a slight wound in my heel from shrapnel. I had a narrow escape in Wednesday's battle at or near Mons, as I was with the transport, and it was surrounded twice.

The last time I made holes in the stable wall, and had a good position for popping them off—and I did, too; but somehow they got to know where we were, and shelled us for three hours. Off went the roof, and off went the roof of other buildings around us. At last a shell exploded and set fire to our cooking apparatus and our stables. We had twenty-two fine horses, and all the transport in this stable yard. We hung on for orders to remove the horses. None came.

At last a shell like a thunderbolt struck the wall, and down came half the stables, and as luck would have it, as we retired—only about six of us—my brother-in-law, the chap you were going to start when we were called up, went to the right and I went to the left. Just then a shell burst high and struck several down in the yard—it was then I got hit—smashed the butt of my rifle, and sent me silly for five minutes. Then I heard a major say, "For yourselves, boys." I looked for my brother-in-law, but he was not to be seen, and I have not heard of him since. During all this time the fire was spreading rapidly. I was told to go back and cut the horses loose. I did so, and some of them got out, but others were burnt to death.

Then God answered my prayer, and I had strength to run through a line of rifle fire over barbed wire covered by a hedge, and managed to get out of rifle range, three hundred yards or four hundred yards away, and then I fell for want of water. I just had about two teaspoonfuls in my bottle, and then I went on struggling my way through hedges to a railway line.

When I got through I saw an awful sight—a man of the Royal Irish with six wounds from shrapnel. He asked me for water, but I had none. I managed to carry him about half a mile, and then found water. I stuck to him though he was heavy and I was feeling weak and tired. I had to carry him through a field of turnips, and half way I slipped and both fell. I then had a look back and could see the fire mountains high.

I then saw one of my own regiment, and called to him to stay with this man while I went for a shutter or a door, which I got, and with the help of two Frenchmen soon got him to a house and dressed him. We were being shelled again from the other end of the village then. We were about fifteen strong, as some slightly wounded came up and some not wounded. We got him away, and then met a company of Cameron Highlanders, and handed him over to them.

I think I marched nearly sixty-three miles, nearly all on one foot, and at last I got a horse and made my way to Mons, where I was put in the train for Havre.

Letter 14.—From Sergeant Taylor, of the R.H.A.:

Our first brush with the enemy was on August 21st, about thirty miles from Mons, but Mons, my goodness, it was just like Brock's benefit at Belle Vue, and you would have thought it was hailing. Of course, we were returning the compliment. The Germans always found the range, which proved they had good maps, yet in their anxiety they tried to fire too many shells, the consequence being that a lot of them were harmless, and they did not give themselves time to properly fuse them. Only on one day—from the 21st to my leaving—did we miss an action. In General French's report you will, no doubt, see where the 5th Brigade accounted for two of the German cavalry regiments, of which only six troopers were taken prisoners; the rest bit the dust. One of these regiments was the lancers, of which the late queen was honorary colonel.

Letter 15.—From Private J. Atkinson, of the Duke of Wellington's West Riding Regiment, to his wife at Leeds;

Talk about a time! I would not like to go through the same again for love or money.

It is not war. It is murder. The Germans are murdering our wounded as fast as they come across them. I gave myself up for done a week last Sunday night, as we were in the thick of the fight at Mons. Our regiment started fighting with 1,009 and finished with 106 and three officers. That made 109, as we just lost 900. It was cruel. At one place we were at there were six streets of the town where all the women were left widows, and were all wearing the widows' weeds. The French regiment that fought there was made up in the town and they got wiped out.

Letter 16.—From Private Robert Robertson, of the Argylls, to his parents at Musselburgh:

The poor Argylls got pretty well hit, but never wavered a yard for all their losses. The Scots Greys are doing great work at the front—in fact they were the means of putting ten thousand Germans to their fate on Sunday morning. I will never forget that day, as our regiment left a town on the French frontier on Saturday morning at 3 o'clock and marched till 3 a.m. on Sunday into a Belgian town. I was about to have an hour in bed, at least a lie down in a shop, when I was wakened to go on guard at the general's headquarters, and while I was on guard a captain of the crack French cavalry came in with the official report of the ten thousand Germans killed.

The Scots Greys, early that morning, had decoyed the Germans right in front of the machine guns of the French, and they just mowed them down. There was no escape for them, poor devils, but they deserve it the way they go on. You would be sorry for the poor Belgian women having to leave their homes with young children clinging to them. One sad case we came across on the roadside was a woman just out of bed two days after giving birth to a child. The child was torn from her breast, and her breast cut off that the infant was sucking. Then the Germans bayoneted the child before the mother's eyes. We did the best we could for her, but she died about six hours after telling us her hardships.

Letter 17.—From Private Whitaker, of the Coldstream Guards:

You thought it was a big crowd that streamed out of the Crystal Palace when we went to see the Cup Final. Well, outside Compiègne it was just as if that crowd came at us. You couldn't miss them. Our bullets ploughed into them, but still they came for us. I was well entrenched, and my rifle got so hot I could hardly hold it. I was wondering if I should have enough bullets, when a pal shouted, "Up, Guards, and at 'em!" The next second he was rolled over with a nasty knock on the shoulder. He jumped up and hissed, "Let me get at them!" His language was a bit stronger than that.

When we really did get the order to get at them we made no mistake, I can tell you. They cringed at the bayonet, but those on our left wing tried to get round us, and after racing as hard as we could for quite five hundred yards we cut up nearly every man who did not run away.

You have read of the charge of the Light Brigade. It was nowt to our cavalry chaps. I saw two of our fellows who were unhorsed stand back to back and slash away with their swords, bringing down nine or ten of the panic-stricken devils. Then they got hold of the stirrup-straps of a horse without a rider, and got out of the melee. This kind of thing was going on all day.

In the afternoon I thought we should all get bowled over, as they came for us again in their big numbers. Where they came from, goodness knows; but as we could not stop them with bullets they had another taste of the bayonet. My captain, a fine fellow, was near to me, and as he fetched them down he shouted, "Give them socks, my lads!" How many were killed and wounded I don't know; but the field was covered with them.

Letter 18.—From a private in the Coldstream Guards to his mother:

First of all I sailed from Southampton on August 12th on a cattle boat called the *Cawdor Castle*. We sailed at 9.30 at night, and after a passage of 14½ hours landed at Le Havre, on the coast of France. We went into camp there, and then left on August 14th, getting into a train, not third class carriages, but cattle trucks. We were on the train eighteen and a half hours, and I was a bit stiff when I got out at a place called Wassigny. Then we marched through pouring rain to a village, where we slept in some barns. The next day being Sunday, August 16th, we got on the march to a place called Grooges, a distance of about nine miles. We stayed there till Thursday.

Then we started to march to get into Belgium. We got there on Sunday, the 23rd, just outside Mons. We dug trenches, from which we had to retire, and then we got into a position, and there I saw the big battle, but could not do anything, because we were with the artillery. We retreated into France, being shelled all the way, and on the Tuesday, the 25th, we marched into Landrecies. We arrived there about one o'clock and were thinking ourselves lucky. We considered we were going to have two days' rest, but about five o'clock the alarm was raised. The Germans got to the front of us and were trying to get in the town. So we fixed our bayonets, doubled up the road, and the fight started.

The German artillery shelled us, and some poor chaps got hit badly. The chap next to me got shot, and I tried to pull him out of the road, so that I could get down in his place, as there was not room for us all in the firing line. We had to lay down behind and wait our chance. I had got on my knees, and just got hold of his leg, when something hit my rifle and knocked it out of my hand, and almost at the same time a bullet went right through my arm. It knocked me over, and I must have bumped my head, for I do not remember any more till I felt someone shaking me. It was the doctor—a brave man, for he came right up amongst the firing to tend the wounded. He bandaged my arm up, and I had to get to hospital, a mile and a half away, as best I could.

The beasts of Germans shelled the building all night long without hitting it. We moved next morning, and by easy stages left for England.

I am going on fine; shall soon be back and at it again I expect. Keep up your spirits, won't you? I believe it was only your prayers at home that guarded me that Tuesday night, simply awful it was.

Letter 19.—From a wounded English officer, in a Belgian hospital, to his mother:

I do not know if this letter will ever get to you or not, but I am writing on the chance that it will. A lot has happened since I last wrote to you. We marched straight up to Belgium from France, and the first day we arrived my company was put on outposts for the night. During the night we dug a few trenches, etc., so did not get much sleep. The next day the Germans arrived, and I will try and describe the fight. We were only advanced troops of a few hundred holding the line of a canal. The enemy arrived about 50,000 strong. We held them in check all day and killed hundreds of them, and still they came. Finally, of course, we retired on our main body.

I will now explain the part I played. We were guarding a railway bridge over a canal. My company held a semicircle from the railway to the canal. I was nearest the railway. A Scottish regiment completed the semicircle on the right of the railway to the canal. The railway was on a high embankment running up to the bridge, so that the Scottish regiment was out of sight of us. We held the Germans all day, killing hundreds, when about five p.m. the order to retire was eventually given. It never reached us, and we were left all alone. The Germans therefore got right up to the canal on our right, hidden by the railway embankment, and crossed the railway. Our people had blown up the bridge before their departure. We found ourselves between two fires, and I realized we had about 2,000 Germans and a canal between myself and my friends.

We decided to sell our lives dearly. I ordered my men to fix bayonets and charge, which the gallant fellows did splendidly, but we got shot down like nine-pins. As I was loading my revolver after giving the order to fix bayonets I was hit in the right wrist. I dropped my revolver, my hand was too weak to draw my sword. This afterwards saved my life. I had not got far when I got a bullet through the calf of my right leg and another in my right knee, which brought me down. The rest of my men got driven round into the trench on our left. The officer there charged the Germans and was killed himself, and nearly all the men were either killed or wounded.

I did not see this part of the business, but from all accounts the gallant men charged with the greatest bravery. Those who could walk the Germans took away as prisoners. I have since discovered from civilians that around the bridge 5,000 Germans were found dead and about 60 English. These 60 must have been nearly all my company, who were so unfortunately left behind.

As regards myself, when I lay upon the ground I found my coat-sleeve full of blood, and my wrist spurting blood, so I knew an artery of some sort must have been cut. The Germans had a shot at me when I was on the ground to finish me off; that shot hit my sword, which I wore on my side, and broke in half just below the hilt; this turned the bullet off and saved my life. I afterwards found that two shots had gone through my field glasses, which I wore on my belt, and another had gone through my coat pocket, breaking my pipe and putting a hole through a small collapsible tin cup, which must have turned the bullet off me.

We lay out there all night for twenty-four hours. I had fainted away from loss of blood, and when I lost my senses I thought I should never see anything again. Luckily I had fallen on my wounded arm, and the arm being slightly twisted I think the weight of my body stopped the flow of blood and saved me. At any rate, the next day civilians picked up ten of us who were still alive, and took us to a Franciscan convent, where we have been splendidly looked after.

All this happened on August 23rd, it is now September 3rd. I am ever so much better, and can walk about a bit now, and in a few days will be quite healed up. It is quite a small hole in my wrist, and it is nearly healed, and my leg is much better; the bullets escaped the bones, so that in a week I shall be quite all right. Unfortunately the Germans are at present in possession of this district, so that I am more or less a prisoner here. But I hope the English will be here in a week, when I shall be ready to rejoin them.

Letter 20.—From W. Hawkins, of the 3rd Coldstream Guards:

I have a nasty little hole through my right arm, but I am one of the lucky ones. My word, it was hot for us. On the Tuesday night when I got my little lot, what I saw put me in mind of a farmer's machine cutting grass, as the Germans fell just like it. We only lost nine poor fellows, and the German losses amounted to 1,500 and 2,000. So you can guess what it was like. As they were shot down others took their place, as there were thousands of them. The best friend is your rifle with the bayonet. But I soon had mine blown to pieces. How it happened I don't know. . . . I got a bullet through the top of my hat. I will bring my hat home and show you. I felt it go through, but it never as much as bruised my head.

I had then no rifle, so I was obliged to keep down my head. The bullets were whirling over me by the hundred. I stopped until they got a bit slower, and then I got up and was trying to pull a fellow away that had been shot through the head when I managed to receive a bullet through my arm. When I looked in the direction of the enemy I could see them coming by the thousand. Off I went.

I bet I should easily have won the mile that night. I got into the hospital at Landricca amid shot and shell, which were flying by as fast as you like. I got my arm done, and was put to bed. All that night the enemy were trying to blow up the hospital, where they had to turn out the lights so that the Germans could not get the correct range. Then we were taken away in R.A.M.C. vans to Guise, where we slept on the station platform after a nice supper which the French provided.

Letter 21.—From Sergeant Griffiths, of the Welsh Regiment, to his parents at Swansea:

The fighting at Mons was terrible, and it was here that our 4th and 5th Divisions got badly knocked, but fought well. Our artillery played havoc with them. About 10 o'clock on Monday we were suddenly ordered to quit, and quick, too, and no wonder. They were ten to one. Then began that retreat which will go down in history as one of the greatest and most glorious retirements over done. Our boys were cursing because our backs were towards them; but when the British did turn, my word, what a game! The 3rd Coldstreams should be named "3rd Cold steels," and no error. Their bayonet charge was a beauty."

Among numerous other such letters that have been published up and down the country is this in which a corporal of the North Lancashire Regiment gives a graphic little picture of his experiences to the *Manchester City News:*

When we got near Mons the Germans were nearer than we expected. They must have been waiting for us. We had little time to make entrenchments, and had to do the digging lying on our stomachs. Only about 300 of the 1,000 I was with got properly entrenched. The Germans shelled us heavily, and I got a splinter in the leg. It is nearly right now, and I hope soon to go back again. We lost fairly heavily, nearly all from artillery fire. Altogether I was fighting for seventy-two hours before I was hit. The German forces appeared to be never-ending. They were round about us like a swarm of bees, and as fast as one man fell, it seemed, there were dozens to take his place.

There is one in which James Scott, reservist, tells his relatives at Jarrow that British soldiers at Mons dropped like logs. The enemy were shot down as they came up, but it was like knocking over beehives—a hundred came up for every one knocked down. He thought the Germans were the worst set of men he had ever seen. Their cavalry drove women and children in front of them in the streets of Mons so that the British could not fire.

A wounded non-commissioned officer of the Pompadours, (the Essex Regiment), whose regiment left Wembley Park a week before the fighting began, says that in the four days' battle commencing at Mons on the Sunday, August 23rd, and lasting until August 26th, they were continually under fire:

We had to beat off several cavalry attacks as well as infantry, and when the trouble seemed to be over the Germans played on us with shrapnel just like turning on a fire hose. Several of our officers were hit on Wednesday. Heavy German cavalry charged us with drawn sabres, and we only had a minute's warning "to prepare to receive cavalry." We left our entrenchments, and rallying in groups, emptied our magazines into them as they drew near. Men and horses fell in confused heaps. It was a terrible sight. Still, on they came. They brought their naked sabres to the engage, and we could distinctly hear their words of command made in that piercing, high tone of voice which the Germans affect.

The enemy had a terrible death roll before their fruitless charge was completed, a thick line of dead and wounded marking the ground over which they had charged. We shot the wounded horses, to put them out of their misery, whilst our ambulances set to work to render aid to the wounded. Our Red Cross men make no distinction. Friend and foe get the same medical treatment, that's where we score over the Germans.

If they had been Uhlans we should not have spared them, as we owe them a grudge for rounding up some Tommies who were bathing. They took their clothes away, and tied the men to trees. We swore to give them a warm time wherever we met them.

A wounded corporal writes:

It looked as if we were going to be snowed under. The mass of men that came at us was an avalanche, and every one of us must have been simply trodden to death and not killed by bullets or shells when our cavalry charged into them on the left wing, not 500 yards from the trench I was in, and cut them up. Our lads did the rest, but the shells afterwards laid low a lot of them.

The following is an extract from a letter received by a gardener from his son:

You complained last year of the swarms of wasps that destroyed your fruit. Well, dad, they were certainly not larger in number than the Germans who came for us. The Germans are cowards when they get the bayonets at them. A young lieutenant, I don't know his name, was one of the coolest men I have ever seen, and didn't he encourage our chaps! I saw him bring down a couple of Germans who were leading half a company.

A fact that stands out continually in these tales of eyewitnesses is the overwhelming numbers in which the Germans were hurled upon them. One says they seemed to be rising up endlessly out of the very ground, and as fast as one mass was shot down another surged into its place; the innumerable horde is compared by various correspondents to "a great big battering-ram," to a gigantic swarm of wasps, to a swarm of bees, to a flock of countless thousands of sheep trying to rush out of a field; to the unceasing pouring of peas out of a sack. It was the sheer mass and weight of this onrush that forced the small British army back on its systematic, triumphant retreat, and probably the most striking little sketch of this phase of the conflict is that supplied by an Irish soldier invalided to Belfast, which I include in the following selection of hospital stories.

A wounded private of the Middlesex Regiment says:

The last few weeks have been like a dream to me. After we landed at Boulogne we were magnificently treated, and everyone was in the highest spirits. Then we set off on our marching. We were all anxious to have a slap at the Germans. My word! If they only knew in our country how the Germans are treating our wounded there would be the devil to pay.

It was somewhere in the neighbourhood of Mons, I believe, that we got our first chance. We had been marching for days with hardly any sleep. When we took up our position the Germans were nearer than we thought, because we had only just settled down to get some rest when there came the blinding glare of the searchlight. This went away almost as suddenly as it appeared, and it was followed by a perfect hail of bullets. We lost a good many in the fight, but we were all bitterly disappointed when we got the order to retire.

I got a couple of bullets through my leg, but I hope it won't be long before I get back again. We never got near enough to use our bayonets. I only wish we had done. Talk about civilised warfare! Don't you believe it. The Germans are perfect fiends.

In Hospital.

(1) At Southampton.

The first batch of wounded soldiers arrived at Netley on the 28th August, coming from Southampton Docks by the hospital train. A *Daily Telegraph* correspondent was one of a quiet band of people who had waited silently for many long hours on the platform that runs alongside the hospital for the arrival of the disabled soldiers who had fought so heroically at Mons; and this is his account of what he saw:

Colonel Lucas and staff were all in readiness. Here were wheeling chairs, there stretchers. The preparations for the reception of the broken Tommies could not have been better, more elaborate, or more humane. It was the humanity of it all—the quiet consideration that told of complete preparedness—that made not the least moving chapter of the story that I have to tell. And out of the train stern-faced men began to hobble, many with their arms in a sling.

Here was a hairless-faced, boyish-looking fellow, with his head enveloped in snowy-white bandages; his cheeks were red and healthy, his eyes bright and twinkling. There was pain written across his young face, but he walked erect and puffed away at a cigarette. One man, with arms half clinging round the neck of two injured comrades, went limping to the reception-room, his foot the size of three, and as he went by he smiled and joked because he could only just manage to get along.

When the last of the soldiers able to walk found his way into the hospital, there to be refreshed with tea or coffee or soup, before he was sent to this or that ward, the more seriously wounded were carried from the train. How patient, how uncomplaining were these fellows! One, stretched out on a mattress, with his foot smashed, chatted and smoked until his turn came to be wheeled away. And when the last of these wounded heroes had been lifted out of the train I took myself to the reception-room, and there heard many stories that, though related with the simplicity of the true soldier, were wonderful.

The wounded men were of all regiments and spoke all dialects. They were travel-stained and immensely tired. Pain had eaten deep lines into many of their faces, but there were no really doleful looks. They were faces that seemed to say: "Here we are; what does it all matter; it is good to be alive; it might have been worse."

I sat beside a private, named Cox. An old warrior he looked. His fine square jaw was black with wire-like whiskers. His eyes shone with the fire of the man who had suffered, so it seemed, some dreadful nightmare.

"And you want me to tell you all about it. Well, believe me, it was just hell. I have been through the Boxer campaign; I went through the Boer War, but I have never seen anything so terrible as that which happened last Sunday. It all happened so sudden. We believed that the Germans were some fifteen miles away, and all at once they opened fire upon us with their big guns.

"Let me tell you what happened to my own regiment. When a roll call of my company was taken there were only three of us answered, me and two others." When he had stilled his emotion, he went on. "So unexpected and so terrible was the attack of the enemy, and so overwhelming were their numbers, that there was no withstanding it."

Before fire was opened a German aeroplane flew over our troops, and the deduction made by Private Cox and several of his comrades, with whom I chatted, was that the aeroplane was used as a sort of index to the precise locality of our soldiers, and, further, that the Germans, so accurate was their gunnery, had been over this particular battlefield before they struck a blow, and so had acquired an intimate knowledge of the country. Trenches that were dug by our men served as little protection from the fire.

Said Cox: "No man could have lived against such a murderous attack. There was a rain of lead, a deluge of lead, and, talk about being surprised, well, I can hardly realise that, and still less believe what happened."

By the side of Cox sat a lean, fair-haired, freckle-faced private. "That's right," he said, by way of corroborating Cox. "They were fair devils," chimed in an Irishman, who later told me that he came from Connemara. "You could do nothing with them, but I say they are no d—— good as riflemen."

"No, they're not, Mike," ventured a youth. "We got within 400 yards of them, and they couldn't hit us."

"But," broke in the man of Connemara, "they are devils with the big guns, and their aim was mighty good, too. If it had not been they wouldn't have damaged us as they have done."

A few yards away was another soldier, also seated in a wheeling chair, with a crippled leg—a big fine fellow he was. He told me his corps had been ambushed, and that out of 120 only something like twenty survived.

On all hands I heard all too much to show that the Battle of Mons was a desperate affair. Two regiments suffered badly, but there was no marked disposition on the part of any of the soldiers with whom I chatted to enlarge upon the happenings of last weekend. Rather would they talk more freely of the awful atrocities perpetrated by the Germans.

"Too awful for words," one said. "Their treatment of women will remain as a scandal as long as the world lasts. We shall never forget; we shall never forgive. I wish I was back again at the front. Englishmen have only got to realise what devilish crimes are being committed by these Germans to want to go and take a hand in the fight. Women were shot, and so were young girls. In fact, it did not seem to matter to the Germans who they killed, and they seemed to take a delight in burning houses and spreading terror everywhere.

"I have got one consolation, I helped to catch four German spies."

(2) At Belfast.

About 120 officers and men arrived in Belfast on August 31st, direct from the Continent. The *Daily Telegraph* local correspondent says:

They were brought here to be near their friends, for the men had been in Ulster for a long time before leaving for the front, being stationed in Belfast and later in Londonderry. They sailed from this city for the theatre of war on August 14th, to the number of 900. It was remarkable to note how many of them were injured in the legs and feet. All were conveyed to the hospital at the Victoria Military Barracks. The men were glad to see Belfast again, but those to whom I spoke will be bitterly disappointed if they do not get another opportunity for paying off their score against the Germans.

One soldier told me a plain straightforward story, without any embellishments. What made his tale doubly interesting was the fact that he spoke with the experience of a veteran, having gone through the South African War.

Where the Germans had the advantage, he said, was in the apparently endless number of reserves.

"No sooner did we dispose of one regiment than another regiment took its place. It just put me in mind of the Niagara Falls—the terrible rush threatening to carry everything before it.

"No force on earth could have withstood that cataract, and the fact that our men only fell back a little was the best proof of their strength. At one stage there were, I am sure, six Germans to every one of us. Yet we held our ground, and would still have held it but for the fact that after we had dealt with the men before us another force came on, using the bodies of their dead comrades as a carpet.

"The South African War was a picnic compared with this, and on the way home I now and again recoiled with horror as I thought of the awful spectacle which was witnessed before we left the front of piled-up bodies of the German dead. We lost heavily, but the German casualties must have been appalling.

"You must remember that for almost twenty-four hours we bore the brunt of the attack, and the desperate fury with which the Germans fought showed that they believed if they were only once past the British forces the rest would be easy. Not only so, but I am sure we had the finest troops in the German Army against us."

On the way out I heard some slighting comments passed on the German troops, and no doubt some of them are not worth much, but those thrown at us were very fine specimens indeed. I do not think they could have been beaten in that respect.

(3) At Birmingham.

About 120 English soldiers who had been wounded in and around Mons arrived in Birmingham on September 1st, and were removed to the new university buildings at Bournbrook, where facilities have been provided for dealing with over 1,000 patients. The contingent was the first batch to arrive. Though terribly maimed, and looking broken and tired, the men were cheerful. About twenty had to be carried, but the majority of them were able to walk with assistance.

In the course of conversation with a *Daily Telegraph* reporter a number of the men spoke of the terrible character of the fighting.

One man said:"The Germans outnumbered us by 100 to one. As we knocked them down, they simply filled up their gaps and came on as before"

One of the Suffolk men stated that very few were injured by shot wounds. Nearly all the mischief was done by shells. The Germans, he said, fired six at a time, and if you missed one you got the others.

One poor fellow, whose head was so smothered in bandages that his features could not be seen, remarked, "We could beat them with bladder-sticks if it were not for the shells, which were appalling. The effect could not be described."

A private of the West Kent Regiment, who was through the Boer War, said there was never anything like the fighting at Mons in South Africa. That was a game of skittles by comparison. He said:

"They came at us in great masses. It was like shooting rabbits, only as fast as you shot one lot down another lot took their place. You couldn't help hitting them. We had plenty of time to take aim, and if we weren't reaching the Bisley standard all the time, we must have done a mighty lot of execution. As to their rifle fire, they couldn't hit a haystack."

A sergeant gunner of the Royal Field Artillery, who was wounded at Tournai, owing to an injury to his jaw was unable to speak, but he wrote on a pad:

"I was on a flank with my gun and fired about sixty rounds in forty minutes. We wanted support and could not get it. It was about 500 English trying to save a flank attack, against, honestly, I should say, 10,000. As fast as you shot them down more came. But for their aeroplanes they would be useless. I was firing for one hour at from 1,500 yards down to 700 yards, so you can tell what it was like."

(4) At London.

All the heroism that has been displayed by British troops in the present war will never be known. A few individual cases may chance to be heard of. Others will be known only to the Recording Angel. Two instances of extraordinary bravery are mentioned by a couple of wounded soldiers lying in the London Hospital in the course of a narrative of their own adventures.

One of them, a splendid fellow of the Royal West Kent Regiment, told a *Daily Telegraph* reporter:

We were in a scrubby position just outside Mons from Saturday afternoon till Monday morning. After four hours each of our six big guns was put out of action. Either the gunners were killed or wounded, or the guns themselves damaged. For the rest of the time—that is, until Monday morning, when we retired—we had to stick the German fire without being able to retaliate. It was bad enough to stand this incessant banging away, but it made it worse not to be able to reply.

All day Sunday and all Sunday night the Germans continued to shrapnel us. At night it was just hellish. We had constructed some entrenchments, but it didn't afford much cover and our losses were very heavy. On Monday we received the order to retire to the south of the town, and some hours later, when the roll-call was called, it was found that we had 300 dead alone, including four officers.

Then an extraordinary thing happened. Me and some of my pals began to dance. We were just dancing for joy at having escaped with our skins, and to forget the things we'd seen a bit, when bang! and there came a shell from the blue, which burst and got, I should think, quite twenty of us.

That's how some of us got wounded, as we thought we had escaped. Then another half dozen of us got wounded this way. Some of our boys went down a street near by, and found a basin and some water, and were washing their hands and faces when another shell burst above them and laid most of them out.

What happened to us happened to the Gloucesters. Their guns, too, were put out of action, and, like us, they had to stand the shellfire for hours and hours before they were told to retire. What we would have done without our second in command I don't know.

During the Sunday firing he got hit in the head. He had two wounds through the cap in the front and one or two behind, and lost a lot of blood. Two of our fellows helped to bind up his head, and offered to carry him back, but he said, "It isn't so bad. I'll be all right soon." Despite his wounds and loss of blood, he carried on until we retired on Monday. Then, I think, they took him off to hospital.

A stalwart chap of the Cheshires here broke in.

Our Cheshire chaps were also badly cut up. Apart from the wounded, several men got concussion of the brain by the mere explosions. It was awful! Under cover of their murderous artillery fire, the German infantry advanced to within three and five hundred yards of our position. With that we were given the order to fix bayonets, and stood up for the charge. That did it for the German infantry! They turned tail and ran for their lives.

Our captain cried out, "Now you've got 'em, men!" But we hadn't. Their artillery begins with that to fire more hellish than ever, and before you could almost think what to do a fresh lots of the "sausages "came along, and we had to beat a retreat.

During the retreat one of our sergeants was wounded and fell. With that our captain runs back and tries to lift him. As he was doing so he was struck in the foot, and fell over. We thought he was done for, but he scrambles up and drags the sergeant along until a couple of us chaps goes out to help 'em in. You should have seen his foot when he took his boot off—I mean the captain. It wasn't half smashed.

How a number of British troops made a dash in the night to save some women and children from the Germans was told by Lance-Corporal Tanner, of the 2nd Oxfordshire and Bucks Light Infantry.

On the Sunday the regiment arrived at Mons.

> We took up our position in the trenches, and fought for some time. In the evening the order came to retire, and we marched back to Conde, with the intention of billeting for the night and having a rest. Suddenly, about midnight, we were ordered out, and set off to march to the village of Douai, some miles away, as news had reached us that the Germans were slaughtering the natives there.
>
> It was a thrilling march in the darkness, across the unfamiliar country. We were liable to be attacked at any moment, of course, but everyone was keen on saving the women and children, and hurried on. We kept the sharpest lookout on all sides, but saw nothing of the enemy.
>
> When we reached Douai a number of the inhabitants rushed out to meet us. They were overjoyed to see us, and speedily told what the Germans had done. They had killed a number of women and children. With fixed bayonets we advanced into the village, and we saw signs all around us of the cruelty of the enemy.

Private R. Wills, of the Highland Light Infantry, who also took part in the march to the village, here continued the story.

> We found that most of the Germans had not waited for our arrival, and there were only a few left in the place. However, we made sure that none remained there.
>
> We started a house-to-house search. Our men went into all the houses, and every now and then they found one or two of the enemy hiding in a corner or upstairs. Many of them surrendered at once, others did not.
>
> When we had cleared the village, some of us lay down on the pavements, and snatched an hour's sleep. At 3.30 we marched away again, having rid the place of the enemy, and, getting back to camp, were glad to turn in.

A sergeant of the Royal Field Artillery, who was wounded by shrapnel just outside Mons village, said that the German artillery-fire was good; once the enemy's gunners got the range they did well.

> Their shooting was every bit as good as ours, and although our battery made excellent practice, three of our men were killed, and twenty out of thirty-six were wounded. I lay on the field

all night, and was rescued the next morning. Fortunately, the Germans did not come and find me during those long hours of loneliness.

In such tales of these men in hospital, and in the letters they have written home, there is a common agreement that the German rifle shooting is beneath contempt—"they shoot from the hip and don't seem to aim at anything in particular;" but their artillery practice is spoken of with respect and admiration. Private Geradine, of the 1st Northumberland Fusiliers writes:

> The German artillery is very good, but their aeroplanes help them a lot. It is a pretty sight to see the shells burst in the night,—it's like Guy Fawkes Day!

I like too, such robust cheerfulness and gay good-humour in face of the horrors of death as sounds through the letter of Sapper Bradley:

> I have never seen our lads so cheery as they are under great trials. You couldn't help being proud of them if you saw them lying in the trenches cracking jokes or smoking while they take pot shots at the Germans. . . . We have very little spare time now, but what we have we pass by smoking concerts, sing-songs, and storytelling. Sometimes we have football for a change, with a German helmet for a ball, and to pass the time in the trenches have invented the game of guessing where the next German shell will drop. Sometimes we have bets on it, and the man who guesses correctly the greatest number of times takes the stakes.

And surely no less do I like the equally courageous but more sombre outlook of the Scottish private who complained of the famous retreat from Mons:

> It was "Retire! retire! retire!" when our chaps were longing to be at them. But they didn't swear about it, because being out there and seeing what we saw makes you feel religious.

I like that wonderful diary kept by a driver of the 4th Ammunition Column, 3rd section, R.F.A. It was sent over from Paris by Mr. Harold Ashton, *The Daily News* correspondent, and is as naively and minutely realistic as if it were a page out of Defoe. The driver's interests are naturally centred in his horses, they hold the first place in his regard, the excitements of the war coming second. He records how he went from Hendon to Southampton on the 21st August:

Got horses on board all right, though the friskiest of them kicked a lot. Got to Havre safe. Food good—rabbit and potatoes and plenty of beer, not our English sort, but the colour of cider. Us four enjoyed ourselves with the family, had a good time, and left ten o'clock next day well filled up. Our objective was Compiègne. We got through all right, watering our horses on the way from pumps and taps at private houses. The people were awful kind, giving us quantities of pears, and filling our water-bottles with beer. That was all right. Our welcome was splendid everywhere.

At Compiègne we got into touch with the Germans. Very hot work. We marched from Compiègne about eleven o'clock on the 31st, which was Sunday. The way was hard. Terrible steep hills which knocked out our older and weaker horses. Collick broke out among them, too, and that was bad. We lost a good many . . . Slept until 5 a.m. and then marched on again, still retreating. Hot as —. Nothing to eat or drink. Plenty of tea, but nothing to boil it with. At last we got some dry biscuits and some tins of marmalade. Bill ——, whose teeth were bad, went near mad with toothache after the jam. . . . No dead horses, thank God, today. I hope we have checked that —— collick, but my horse fell into a ditch going through the wood and could not get out for over an hour.

I couldn't go for help, because the Germans had got the range of the place and their shells were ripping overhead like blazes. Poor old Dick (the horse), he was that fagged out by the long march. At last I got him out and went on, and by luck managed to pick up my pals. . . . The Germans were lambing in at us with their artillery, and poor old Dick got blowed up. I thank God I wasn't on him just then.

Sept. 2.—More fighting and worser than ever. I don't believe we shall ever get to Paris. . . . Now we come to Montagny, and fighting all the time. Rabbits and apples to eat gallore, but still no money, and no good if we had because we carnt spend it.

Sept. 3.—We progressed this day four miles in twelve hours. Took the wrong road, and had to crawl about the woods on our stummoks like snakes to dodge the German snipers. We had one rifle between four of us, and took it in turns to have goes.

We shot one blighter and took another prisoner. They was both half starved and covered with soars. Then the rifle jammed, and we had nothing to defend ourselves with. At last we found the main body again. They wanted more horses, and we were just bringing them up and putting them to the guns when a German areyplane came over us and flue round pretty low. The troops tried to fetch him down, and some bullets went through the wings, but then he got too high. He dropped a bomb in the middle of us, but it exploded very weak and nobody was hurt. Next day we started on a night march, and got to Lagny Thorigny, and camped outside the town, where the people fed us on rabbits again. I said I was sick of rabbits, and me and Bill walked acrost to a farmhouse and borrowed three chickens, which we cooked. It was fine. . . . Outside Lagny there was more fierce fighting—20 miles of it—and the Germans were shot down like birds.

Sept. 3 (continued).—Firing is still going on, but it is not so fierce, though scouts have come in and told us there are 10,000 Germans round us this day. Tonight I got two ounces of Navy Cut. It was prime.

Sept. 8.—We are marching on further away from Paris. We shall never get there, I guess.

Sept. 12.—In the village of Crecy. Plenty of food and houses to sleep into. Here we have got to stay until further orders. Collick still very bad.

The calm matter-of-fact air with which he encounters whatever comes to him, the keen joy he takes in small pleasures by the way; his philosophic acceptance of the fate of "poor old Dick"—the whole thing is so unruffled, so self-possessed, so Pepysian in its egoism and so artlessly humorous that one hopes this phlegmatic driver will keep a full diary of his campaignings, and that Mr. Ashton will secure and publish it.

3

The Destruction of Louvain

"Such food a tyrant's appetite demands."
Wordsworth.

The stupid arrogance of the German military caste has always made them ridiculous in the eyes of decent human creatures; it was surprising, amusing, and yet saddening, too, to see an intelligent people strutting and playing such war-paint-and-feathers tricks before high heaven, but it appears that the primitive impulses that survive in their character are stronger and go deeper than we had suspected. There are brave and chivalrous spirits among Germany's officers and men; that goes without saying; but the savage and senseless barbarities that have marked her conduct of the present war will make her name a byword for infamy as long as it is remembered.

There seems no doubt—the charges are too many and too widely spread—that her troops have murdered the wounded, have shot down women and children, have even used them as shields, driving them in front of their firing line; they have ruthlessly murdered unarmed civilians, and have blasted farmsteads and villages into ashes on the flimsiest provocation; sometimes, so far as one can learn, without waiting for any provocation whatever. Even if their hands were clean of that innocent blood, the wanton, insensate destruction of such a city as Louvain is sufficient of itself to put them outside the pale of civilised societies.

No doubt they were smarting with humiliation that they had been so long delayed breaking through the stubborn opposition of the Belgians at Liège; but Louvain was an unfortified city and they were allowed to take peaceable possession of it. Nevertheless, on August 25th whilst the fighting round Mons was at its hottest and Russia was sweeping farther and farther over the frontiers of East Prussia, in some sort of burst of vengeful frenzy they laid one of the loveliest old cities of the world in ruins, burnt or shattered most of its priceless art treasures, and left its citizens homeless. Of course they have been busy ever since trying to cover up their shame with excuses, but such a wanton crime is too great and too glaringly obvious to be hidden or excused.

Four impressively realistic descriptions of what happened when the Germans thus went mad in Louvain have been published in the *Daily Telegraph*:

1. From a *Daily Telegraph* Folkestone Correspondent, Saturday, August 29th:

> Among the refugees arriving here today were women and children from Louvain and soldiers from Liège, all narrating thrilling adventures. Some of the refugees had obviously hurriedly deserted their homes, wrapping a few of their belongings in sheets of newspaper.
>
> One woman from Louvain tore down the curtains from her windows, wrapped them round some wearing apparel, and ran from her house with her two children. In the street she became involved in a stampede of men, women, and children tearing away from the burning town, whither she knew not. This woman's story was so disjointed, so interspersed with hysterical sobs and exclamations, that it is impossible to make a full and coherent narrative of it. Periodically she clasped her children, gazed round upon the English faces, and thanked God and bemoaned her fate alternately.
>
> Although suffering from extreme nervous excitement, another woman had intervals of comparative calmness during which she described her experiences as follows:
>
> "*Ah! m'sieu*," she exclaimed, "I will tell you, yes, of the burning of Louvain. We had pulled down some of the buildings so that the Germans should not mount guns on them when they came. I believe that was the reason. We were in a state of terror because we had heard of the cruelties of the Germans."
>
> Every time the poor woman referred to the Germans she paused to utter maledictions upon them.
>
> "Well," she proceeded, "they came, and all we had heard about them was not so bad as we experienced. In the streets people

49

were cruelly butchered, and then on all sides flames began to rise. We were prepared for what we had regarded as the worst, but never had we anticipated that they would burn us in our homes.

"People rushed about frantic to save their property. Pictures of relatives were snatched from the walls, clothing was seized, and the people were demented.

"What was the excuse given? Well, they said our people had shot at them, but that was absolutely untrue. The real reason was the pulling down of the buildings. My house was burning when I left it with my three children, and here I am with them safe in England, beautiful England. But what we have suffered! We were part of a crowd which left the burning town, and kept walking without knowing where we were going. Miles and miles we trudged, I am told we walked over seventy miles before we came to a railway. I never regarded a railway as I did then. I wanted to bow down and kiss the rails. I fell exhausted, having carried my children in turn. Footsore, broken-hearted, after the first joy of sighting the railway, I felt my head whirling, and I wondered whether it was all worth while. Then I thought of my deliverance, and thanked God.

"What did Louvain look like? Like what it was, a mass of flame devouring our homes, our property—to some, perhaps, our relatives. It was pitiful to behold. Most of us women were deprived of our husbands. They had either fallen or were fighting for their country. In the town everybody who offered any opposition was killed, and everyone found to be armed in any way was shot. Wives saw their husbands shot in the streets.

"I saw the *burgomaster* shot, and I saw another man dragged roughly away from his weeping wife and children and shot through the head. Well, we got a train and reached Boulogne, and now for the first time we feel really safe."

2. From a *Daily Telegraph* Rotterdam correspondent, Sunday, August 30th.

The following account of the appalling and ruthless sacking of Louvain by the Germans is given by a representative of the *Nieuwe Rotterdamsche Courant*, who himself witnessed the outrages:

I arrived at Louvain on Tuesday afternoon, and, accompanied by a German officer, made my way through the town. Near the station were the commander and staff and many of the military, for a food and ammunition train had just arrived. Suddenly shots rang out from houses in the neighbourhood of the station. In a moment the shooting was taken up from houses all over the town.

From the window of the third floor of an hotel opposite the station a machine gun opened fire. It was impossible to know which of the civilians had taken part in the shooting, and from which houses they had fired. Therefore the soldiers went into all the houses, and immediately there followed the most terrible scenes of street fighting. Every single civilian found with weapons, or suspected of firing, was put to death on the spot. The innocent suffered with the guilty.

There was no time for exhaustive inquiry. Old men, sick people, women were shot. In the meanwhile, part of the town was shelled by artillery. Many buildings were set on fire by the shells. On others petrol was poured and a match applied. The German officer advised me to go away, as several houses being still intact more firing was expected.

Under a strong escort two groups of men and women arrived, each a hundred strong. They were hostages. They were stood in rows by the station, and every time a soldier was shot in the town ten of these pitiful civilians were slaughtered. There was no mercy. Tears and pleadings were in vain. The good suffered with the bad. At night the scene was terrible, burning buildings shedding a lurid glow over this town, which was running with tears of blood.

This was no time for sleep. The sight of this terrible awfulness drove away all thoughts and desire for rest. Towards dawn the soldiers took possession of all buildings which had not been destroyed.

With the rising of the sun I walked on the boulevards, and saw them strewn with bodies, many of them being of old people and priests. Leaving Louvain for Tirlemont one passed continuously through utterly devastated country.

A Dutchman who escaped from Louvain says that when the German artillery began to demolish the houses and the German soldiers began looting everything he and his little son hid in a cellar beneath a pile of pneumatic tyres. One woman took refuge in a pit, in which water was up to her waist. Such was the terrible plight of the civilians in Louvain. Peeping out they saw that neighbours had been driven to the roof of a burning building, where they perished.

While still concealed in the cellar the Dutchman and his son discovered to their horror that the house above them was in flames. The situation was terrible, as the people who dared to leave their houses were shot like rabbits leaving burrows. They heard floor by floor, and then the roof, crash down above them. The situation was desperate. It was impossible to remain in the cellar. Driven out by dire necessity, they fled. They were immediately stopped by military rifles at the "present."

"Do not fire, I am German," said the Dutchman in German, seized with a sudden inspiration. This secured his safe conduct to the railway station. The journey through the town was, said this refugee, "like walking through hell." From burning houses he heard agonised cries of those perishing in the conflagrations. While he was waiting at the station fifty people arrived there, driven by troops, who asserted that they found them hiding in houses from which shots had been fired. These people swore by all they held sacred they were innocent, but notwithstanding all were shot. The Dutchman is of opinion that the first firing was not by civilians, but by the German outpost on German soldiers retreating to Louvain from Malines.

Note:—There is no confirmation whatever of the Dutch correspondent's assertion with regard to the firing on the German troops. On the contrary it has been expressly said by the Belgian Government that the Germans fired on their own men by mistake.

3. From a *Daily Telegraph* Rotterdam Correspondent, Monday, August 31st:

An escaped Dutchman said to a *Nieuwe Rotterdamsche Courant* representative:

> With a crowd of other men, I was marched out of Louvain, and at nightfall ordered into a church. All was dark, till suddenly, through the windows, I saw the lurid glow of the neighbouring burning houses. I heard the agonised cries of people tortured by the flames. Six priests moved among us, giving absolution. Next morning the priests were shot—why, I know not. We were released, and allowed to go to Malines. We were compelled to walk with our hands in the air for fear of arms being concealed.

GERMAN SOLDIERS DRIVING THE INHABITANTS OF LOUVAIN BEFORE
THEM DURING THE SACKING OF THE TOWN.

A Dutchman who has arrived at Breda from Louvain gives the *Nieuwe Rotterdamsche Courant* the following account of the massacre:

> Several German soldiers were billeted on us, and just as we were sitting down to the midday meal on August 25th the alarm was sounded and the soldiers rushed out. Immediately firing started, and, knowing the terrible consequences of civilians appearing in the streets at such times, we sought refuge in the cellar. Next morning we attempted to reach the railway station. We were arrested.
>
> My wife was taken away from me, and the mayor, the principal of the university, and I, with other men, were taken to a goods shed and our hands bound. I saw 300 men and boys marched to the corner of the Boulevarde van Tienen, and every one was massacred. The heads of police were shot. We were then marched towards Herent, and on the way the soldiers thought the enemy was approaching, and ordered us to kneel down. Then they took cover behind us. Only after many such hardships were we permitted to return, to Louvain and escape by train.

4. From a *Daily Telegraph* Rotterdam correspondent, Wednesday, September 2nd:

A Dutchman who has just arrived at Breda from Louvain gives the following vivid description of his terrible experiences in Louvain, where he was present at the burning of the city:

> We Dutchmen in Louvain at first had nothing to fear from the German soldiers, but all the houses abandoned by their owners were ransacked, notwithstanding the warnings from the military authorities forbidding the troops to pillage. In Louvain, as in all other towns they have occupied, the Germans imprisoned as hostages of war the Burgomaster, two magistrates, and a number of influential citizens.
>
> Before the Germans entered the town the Civic Guard had been disarmed, and all weapons in the possession of the population had to be given up. Even toy guns and toy pistols and precious collections of old weapons, bows and arrows, and other antique arms useless for any kind of modern warfare had to be surrendered, and all these things—sometimes of great personal value to the owner—have since been destroyed by the Germans. The value of one single private collection has been

estimated at about £1,000. From the pulpits the priests urged the people to keep calm, as that was the only way to prevent harm being done to them.

A few days after the entry of the German troops, the military authorities agreed to cease quartering their men in private houses, in return for a payment of 100,000 *francs* (£4,000) per day. On some houses between forty and fifty men had been billeted. After the first payment of the voluntary contribution the soldiers camped in the open or in the public buildings. The beautiful rooms in the Town Hall, where the civil marriages take place, were used as a stable for cavalry horses.

At first everything the soldiers bought was paid for in cash or promissory notes, but later this was altered. Soldiers came and asked for change, and when this was handed to them they tendered in return for the hard cash a piece of paper—a kind of receipt.

On Sunday, the 23rd, I and some other influential people in the town were roused from our beds. We were informed that an order had been given that 250 mattresses, 200 lbs. of coffee, 250 loaves of bread, and 500 eggs, must be on the market-place within an hour. On turning out we found the *burgomaster* standing on the market-place, and crowds of citizens, half naked, or in their night attire, carrying everything they could lay hands on to the market, that no harm might befall their *burgomaster*. After this had been done the German officer in command told us that his orders had been misinterpreted, and that he only wanted the mattresses.

On Tuesday, the 25th, many troops left the town. We had a few soldiers in our house. At six o'clock, when everything was ready for dinner, alarm signals sounded, and the soldiers rushed through the streets, shots whistled through the air, cries and groans arose on all sides; but we did not dare leave our house, and took refuge in the cellar, where we stayed through long and fearful hours. Our shelter was lighted up by the reflection from the burning houses. The firing continued unceasingly, and we feared that at any moment our houses would be burnt over our heads. At break of day I crawled from the cellar to the street door, and saw nothing but a raging sea of fire.

At nine o'clock the shooting diminished, and we resolved to make a dash to the station. Abandoning our home and all our goods except what we could carry, and taking all the money we had, we rushed out. What we saw on our way to the station is hardly describable, everything was burning, the streets were covered with bodies shot dead and half-burnt. Everywhere proclamations had been posted, summoning every man to assist in quenching the flames, and the women and children to stay inside the houses. The station was crowded with fugitives, and I was just trying to show an officer my legitimation papers when the soldiers separated me from my wife and children.

All protests were useless, and a lot of us were marched off to a big shed in the goods yard, from where we could see the finest buildings of the city, the most beautiful historical monuments, being burned down.

Shortly afterwards German soldiers drove before them 300 men and lads to the corner of the Boulevard van Tienen and the Maria Theresia Street, opposite the Café Vermalen. There they were shot. The sight filled us with horror. The *burgomaster*, two magistrates, the rector of the university, and all police officials had been shot already.

With our hands bound behind our backs we were then marched off by the soldiers, still without having seen our wives or children. We went through the Juste de Litsh Street, along the Diester Boulevard, across the Vaart and up the hill.

From the Mont Cesar we had a full view of the burning town, St. Peter in flames, while the troops incessantly sent shot after shot into the unfortunate town. We came through the village of Herent—one single heap of ruins—where another troop of prisoners, including half-a-dozen priests, joined us. Suddenly, about ten o'clock, evidently as the result of some false alarm, we were ordered to kneel down, and the soldiers stood behind us with their rifles ready to fire, using us as a shield. But fortunately for us nothing happened.

After a delay of half-an-hour, our march was continued. No conversation was allowed, and the soldiers continually maltreated us. One soldier struck me with all his might with the heavy butt-end of his rifle. I could hardly walk any further, but I had to. We were choked with thirst, but the Germans wasted their drinking water without offering us a drop.

At seven o'clock we arrived at Camperhout, *en route* for Malines. We saw many half-burnt dead bodies—men, women, and children. Frightened to death and half-starved, we were locked up in the church, and there later joined by another troop of prisoners from the surrounding villages.

At ten o'clock the church was lighted up by burning houses. Again shots whistled through the air, followed by cries and groans.

At five o'clock next morning, all the priests were taken out by the soldiers and shot, together with eight Belgian soldiers, six cyclists, and two gamekeepers. Then the officer told us that we could go back to Louvain. This we did, but only to be recaptured by other soldiers, who brought us back to Camperhout. From there we were marched to Malines, not by the high road, but along the river. Some of the party fell into the water, but all were rescued. After thirty-six hours of ceaseless excitement and danger we arrived at Malines, where we were able to buy some food, and from there I escaped to Holland. I still do not know where my wife and children are.—*Reuter's Special Service.*

So far as available evidence goes, it seems clear enough that by some misunderstanding the German soldiers fired upon each other in the town, and then made the unhappy townsfolk pay the price of their tragic blundering. There are hopes that the beautiful old Hotel de Ville escaped the general holocaust; otherwise Louvain and its ancient glories of art and architecture are things of the past.

The well-known French novelist, Romain Roland, in an open letter addressed to the German dramatist, Gerhart Hauptmann writes:

Louvain is no longer anything but a heap of cinders. . . . In the name of Europe, of which you have till now been one of the most illustrious champions, in the name of civilisation, for which the greatest of men have been fighting for centuries—in the name of the very honour of the Germanic race, I adjure you, Gerhart Hauptmann, and the German intellectual elite, among whom I count so many friends, to protest against this crime. If you do not, it can only mean one of two things, either that you approve, or that you are impotent to raise your voice against the Huns who rule you. In the latter case, how can you still pretend that you are fighting for the cause of human liberty and progress? . . . Are you the descendants of Goethe, or of Attila?

4

The Fight in the North Sea

Strong Mother of a Lion line,
Be proud of these strong sons of thine.
                              Tennyson.

In the three weeks that followed on the declaration of war, tidings came to us from time to time of how our ships were chasing and sinking the enemy's cruisers, capturing his merchantmen and keeping the ocean-highways clear for our own and neutral commerce; but no word reached us from the great British fleet that was keeping watch and ward in the North Sea, waiting sleeplessly for the German Navy that was sheltered behind the impregnable fort of Heligoland to dash out and make its loudly threatened raid upon our coasts. We heard no word of those guardian sailormen, but we slept peacefully in our beds at night, confident in their strength, their courage, their alertness.

Then suddenly, on the 28th August, whilst the British and French armies were in the heat of their strategic retreat from Mons, news of our seamen's dashing fight and victory in the North Sea flashed through the land. They had grown weary of waiting, and as the German was too discreet to venture forth to the attack they had slipped into his fastness under cover of the dark and hunted him out. Until it is possible to compile a connected, orderly narrative, the tale of that brilliant engagement is best told in the letters of the men who had part in it:

Letter 22.—From Albert Roper, first-class petty officer of H.M. cruiser *Talbot*, to his brother at Leeds:

I cannot give you any news about our movements. It is against the rules to do so, and it's a jolly good job, too, for if it was not so, things would leak out, and that is just what we do not want. We are waiting patiently for Willie's fleet to come out to enable our chaps to have a little practice. We try to make ourselves as happy as we can in the shape of a sing-song occasionally. These evenings are well appreciated.

Letter 23.—From Seaman Wilson, of the *Bacchante*, to his wife at Hunslet:

You will have read of our victory in the North Sea. It was fine. Our ship brought the dead and wounded and the prisoners back. A grim job it was, too. I only wish the whole German fleet would come out. We may get a chance of coming home soon. Their firing is rotten, whilst our men behind the guns are perfect. They get a hit every time.

The bounders won't come out. That was the reason our ships had to try and drive them out. You see the place is all mined, and if a ship runs into one of these mines it means destruction.

The commander of the *Liberty*, a torpedo boat destroyer, asked his ship's company if they would volunteer to go up Kiel Harbour with him, and every man said "Yes," although it looked certain death. Up they went, and got under the forts of Heligoland and let rip at the German cruisers in the harbour. One of the wounded sailors of the *Liberty* told me that the shells fired at them were enough to sink a fleet. Our ship had only one torpedo and one round of ammunition left. So they turned round to come out, when a shrapnel shell struck the *Liberty's* mast, killing the gallant commander and three others. The coxswain, although wounded, brought the ship safely to our fleet that was waiting outside. We pray to God that we may come off victorious, and I am confident we shall, as every man jack in the fleet has the heart of a lion.

Letter 24.—From a Welsh gunner on the *Arethusa*:

Just a few lines to let you know how the war is going on. I cannot say much, as correspondence is strictly secret and letters are likely to be opened. The commodore turned over to this ship last Wednesday, and we were in action on Friday at 7.45 a.m. and finished a stiff eight-hours' engagement, our loss being eleven killed and fifteen injured in this ship alone.

We were done after the fight, engines disabled, and had to be towed to Chatham. One man was all that was left at my gun. But still, after all, we saw them off. We blew them to ——. Three fights we had. As soon as we are patched up we shall be off again.

Letter 25.—From Gunner John Meekly, of Leeds:

Been in battle, and, wonder of wonders, haven't scored a scratch. My ship, as you know, is the *Arethusa*—"Saucy *Arethusa*" as history knows her. She was the first there, and the first that shot home. It was her that made them come out, and her that took the most prominent part, as all the ship's company know only too well. Now we are in dry dock.

We had to sacrifice ourselves almost to do what we did do— to get them out of their shells. Not only were submarines and mines a menace, but also the fire from the forts. We got within their range, and our ship suffered the most. We have got a fearless admiral, and at the same time a decent fellow.

I saw an account in the papers when we got in dock, and I was very pleased with it, because another ship had been mistaken for us. The name of our commodore is Tyrwhitt.

Letter 26.—From Midshipman Hartley, of H.M. battle-cruiser *Lion*, to his parents at Burton-on-Trent:

At last we have had a taste of gunfire, but it was only a taste. We ran into three light German cruisers. Two of them were sunk, and one managed to make of in a sinking condition and badly on fire forward and aft. Of course, their guns had about the same effect on us as a daisy air-rifle. The funny thing, which you should have seen, was all the stokers grubbing about after the action looking for bits of shell.

The Germans fought awfully well and bravely, but the poor beggars hadn't a dog's chance of living through it. The *Mainz* was the name of one of those sunk. Two of their destroyers were also sunk.

Letter 27.—From a Scottish seaman (Published in *The Scotsman*):

It was a sight worth seeing. We chased two German destroyers of the "S" class, one of which went on fire, and the other was sunk by eight British destroyers, including the *Defender*. We chased them for about four hours, and one showed great pluck as the crew refused to haul down the flag, and she sank with the German flag flying. When she sank, and even before it, the sailors were swimming towards the British ships, shouting in broken English that they had surrendered, and appealing for help. It was a terrible sight to see the wounded in the water, and we assisted in throwing out lifebelts and ropes to them, while the whaler and a skiff were also lowered, together with small boats from the other British vessels. While engaged in picking up the wounded and other survivors, we were fired on by a big four-funnelled German cruiser, so that we had to leave our two boats. We watched the cruiser firing seven or eight 11-inch guns, which made us keep going well ahead to keep out of the way.

A piece of shell struck one of the gun's crew on the head, and dropped at my feet, and we had to keep dodging the shells round the bridge. A light cruiser at last came to the rescue, for the destroyer's guns were no use against those of the Germans. Our cruiser sank the German cruiser, and a good many of the enemy's boats escaped. About 12 o'clock on Saturday one of the latest submarines signalled that she had saved the boat's crew (9 men and 1 officer) while following the big cruiser to torpedo her. It was believed these fellows had been lost, and their mates on board never dreamt of seeing them again.

Some German survivors were put aboard a destroyer, and they were cheered by the British tars who were anxious to hear the news from them. A German stoker said they did not want to fight England, and it was too much Germany fighting so many countries. It was terrible to hear the cries of the wounded in the water, and we did not get a chance to pick them up. The men on the sinking destroyer stuck to their guns to the last, and they were firing at their own men who dived for our ships. Some had lifebelts on, and the officers tried to frighten them by saying the British would put them in front of their guns. We had only two hurt.

Letter 28.—From a gun-room officer on H.M, battle-cruiser *Invincible*, to his parents at Hove:

The particular ship we were engaged with was in a pitiful plight when we had finished with her. Her funnels shot away, masts tottering, great gaps of daylight in her sides, smoke and flame

RESCUED BY SUBMARINE.
A STRANGE INCIDENT DURING THE NAVAL ACTION OFF HELIGOLAND.

belching from her everywhere. She speedily heeled over and sank like a stone, stern first. So far as is known none of her crew was saved. She was game to the last, let it be said, her flag flying till she sank, her guns barking till they could bark no more. Although we suffered no loss we had some very narrow escapes. Three torpedoes were observed to pass us, one, it is said, within a few feet. Four-inch shells, too, fell short, or were ahead of us. The sea was alive with the enemy's submarines, which, however, luckily did no damage. They should not be under-rated, these Germans. They've got "guts." That cruiser did not think apparently of surrender.

Letter 29.—From a Bluejacket in the North Sea, to his friends at Jarrow;

On August 24th we made a dash for the German coast and were lucky enough to come across two German cruisers. Then the fun started. We pursued one, and when I tell you we can do thirty knots, you can imagine what chance she had of getting away. She was a heavier boat than us, and the engagement lasted four hours. At the end of that time she was a terrible sight. She was on fire from stem to stem; the Germans were jumping overboard, and at the finish only seventeen out of 400 were saved. It is a fact that the Germans only stayed at their guns under the orders of their officers, who stood over them with revolvers. Three dozen of their bodies, which were picked up, bore marks of revolver shots. Five days every week for the last four weeks we have swept the North Sea, and all we discovered were the aforesaid two cruisers and about a dozen trawlers, which we sank. There is no sign of the big German Navy. They are in Kiel Harbour, and if they come out—well, there will be no German Navy left. The only things they are using are mines and submarines. In fact, the so-called German Navy is a "wash-out."
We have been within ten miles of their base and they will not come out.

Letter 30.—From Seaman-Gunner Brown, to his parents at Newport, Isle of Wight;

We and another ship in our squadron came across two German cruisers. We outed one and started on the second, but battle-cruisers soon finished her off. Another then appeared, and after we had plunked two broadsides into her she slid off in flames. Every man did his bit, and there was a continuous stream of jokes. We pencilled on the projectiles. "Love from England," "One for the *Kaiser*," and other such messages.

The sight of sinking German ships was gloriously terrible; funnels and masts lying about in all directions, and amidships a huge furnace, the burning steel looking like a big ball of sulphur. There was not the slightest sign of fear, from the youngest to the oldest man aboard.

Letter 31.—From a man in a warship's engine-room:

We stayed down there keeping the engines going at their top speed in order to cut off the Germans from their fleet. We could hear the awful din and the scampering of the tars on the deck as they rushed about from point to point. We could hear the shells crashing against the side of the ship or shrieking overhead as they passed harmlessly into the water, and we knew that at any moment one might strike us in a vital part, and send us below never to come up again. It is ten times harder on the men whose duty is in the engine-room than for those on deck taking part in the fighting, for they at least have the excitement of the fight, and if the ship is struck they have more than a sporting chance of escape. We have none, and the medals and pats on the back when the fight is won are not for us, who are only common mechanics.

Letter 32.—From Seaman Jack Diggett, of West Bromwich, to his brother:

You will have heard of our little job in the North Sea. We sank five ships and ran a few off. Of course it was only a trial spin. We kicked off last Friday about six in the morning, and we won 5—nil. Not bad, considering we are playing "away." Their goalkeepers could not hold us, we were so hot. Our forwards shot beautifully, and our defence was sound. We agreed to play extra time if we had not finished, but we had done in time. It must not be thought that we had it all our own way, for they were very brave, and fought until one of our boys fired a shot at the last gun in the *Mainz* and blew the whole gun and crew as well into the sea. One of our officers had both his legs blown off, and still shouted out to give the Germans another. We are all getting ready for the big match of the season now when their battle fleet chooses to come out. One German officer we got out of the water asked, "Are you British?" When our officer replied, "Yes," he said, "God help us!" They thought we were the French fleet.

Letter 33.—From a seaman on H.M.S. *Hearty*:

The destroyer *Laurel* seems to have suffered the most. She had one funnel carried right away and the others riddled like a pepper-box. One shell struck her right forward, went through her bulkhead, through one galley door, and out through the other. The cookie was in there at the time, but it missed him and cut through the other side of the ship. That cook was born under a lucky star. It's on the bridge and around the guns where they suffered most. On the *Liberty's* bridge, everybody except one was killed; in fact they say they were never seen since. Poor devils, they must have been carried right overboard. The skipper of the *Laurel* had both his legs shot away.
The scout *Arethusa* came in last. She brought 100 Germans picked up oft the cruiser *Mainz*, We didn't see them; they were landed down at Sheerness. They've got one keepsake off her. They picked up a German officer, but he died, and they buried him at sea. They've got his uniform hanging up. The cooks on the *Arethusa* were not so lucky. Two cooks were in the galley, just having their rum, when a shell killed one and blew the other's arm off. A funny thing, they've got a clock hanging up; it smashed the glass and one hand, but the blooming thing's still going.

Letter 34.—From a seaman on H.M, destroyer *Lurcher*, to a friend at Bradford:

We had orders to pick up prisoners. As we steamed up dead bodies were floating past the ship. We went up alongside the German cruiser *Mainz* just before she sank, and it was an awful sight. We got 224 prisoners in a most terrible state, and most of them died. It is impossible to describe it all on paper. Our decks were red with blood, and you see we are only a destroyer, so you may tell what a mess we were in.
All the Germans seemed quite happy when we got them on

board. The worst job of all was getting them out of the sea. Some of them had legs and arms shot away, battered to pieces. I was in our boat just below when their vessel sank, and there seemed to be many who were helpless on board her. The captain remained behind, having had both legs shot away.

Letter 35.—From a naval lieutenant to a friend:

That was all. Remains only little details, only one of which I will tell you. The most romantic, dramatic, and piquant episode that modern war can ever show. The *Defender*, having sunk an enemy, lowered a whaler to pick up her swimming survivors; before the whaler got back an enemy's cruiser came up and chased the *Defender*, and thus she abandoned her whaler. Imagine their feelings—alone in an open boat without food, 25 miles from the nearest land, and that land the enemy's fortress, with nothing but fog and foes around them.

Suddenly a swirl alongside and up, if you please, pops his Britannic Majesty's submarine E 4, opens his conning tower, takes them all on board, shuts up again, dives, and brings them home 250 miles! Is not that magnificent? No novel would dare face the critics with an episode like that in it, except, perhaps, Jules Verne; and all true!

Letter 36.—From a seaman on one of the British destroyers:

We have at last had an innings at the Germans. It was a go. Fully seven hours we fought shot for shot. I had the pleasure of seeing four German ships go down. We never knew but it might be our turn next, as great shells were falling all around us. Several shells went just over our heads, whistling just like a needle on a broken record. Would you believe it, one of our boats had actually stopped to pick up German wounded when the Germans fired on her?

I think all our men took it just as though we were having our annual battle practice—cool, laughing, and cracking jokes, with shell all around them. All the thought was just of shooting it into them—and they got it! I was told they lost 1,500 men. I shall never understand how it was our ship was not hit, for we were within range of their cruisers and the Heligoland forts. We are ready for another smack at them.

Letter 37.—From a seaman on H.M,S, *New Zealand* to his uncle in Halifax:

The torpedo craft had rather a hot time with the enemy in the early morning, but suddenly we appeared out of the mist. To say that they were surprised is to put it mildly, because before they knew where they were we were playing our light cruisers, and the destroyers worried them like terriers. Then for us to come along and give them the *coup de grace* was absolutely *It*,

Two of their ships, I am convinced, would have been floating today, but as our small ships gathered round them to take off their survivors—all their flags were struck—they opened fire, only to be sent to Davy Jones's locker a little quicker than they could shoot. Well, we succeeded in sending some good ships and some unfortunate men to the bottom in something like fourteen minutes. Not a bad score for the cricket season, is it?

Letter 38.—From a seaman on board the flagship of the first destroyer squadron, to his friends at Wimbledon;

We had a very decent splash last week öff Heligoland, as doubtless you have read. Our ship was not hit at all, though some shots were pretty near. It was a fine sight to see the *Lion* demolish one cruiser. We could see her (the cruiser's) shots falling short, but still the *Lion* did not fire. For fully ten minutes the cruiser belted away without getting a hit. Then the *Lion*, who was leading the line, hoisted "open fire," turned slowly and majestically round and fired her broadside—once. It was quite sufficient. Up went a cloud of smoke and steam from the target, and when it cleared her aft funnel was at a rakish angle, and a huge rent appeared the length of her side.

After a few more "salvoes" she was rapidly sinking by the stern. Shortly afterwards she half-hauled down her ensign, and as we were steaming up to stand by and rescue her survivors, she hoisted it again and opened fire. It was a dirty trick, but they got their deserts. Once again the *Lion* turned, and this time fired but five shots from her huge turrets. Amidst a shower of splinters, smoke, and fire she disappeared. We steamed over the spot, but although there was plenty of wreckage, not a single living thing was to be seen. This incident only lasted about forty-five minutes, although the whole battle was raging for eight hours.

Letter 39.—From leading telegraphist H. Francis, of Croydon:

We had the first taste of blood on Friday, and I can tell you it was O.T. The battle lasted from 6.30 a.m. till one p.m., going at it hammer and tongs all the time.

We came back with sixty prisoners, one of them being Admiral von Tirpitz's son, who was second-lieutenant in the *Mainz*. We were within twenty yards of her when she went down, and I can tell you it was a grand sight.

Their officers were shooting the men as they jumped overboard, and one chap on the bridge was beckoned to by our commander to come off. But there was "nothing doing." He simply folded his arms, shook his head, and as the ship rolled over he never moved. The captain also went down in her. He had both his legs blown off. For a quarter of an hour the sea was simply alive with Germans, all singing out most piteously, and, as we pulled them on board, we marvelled how they managed to swim with the wounds they had, some with feet off, some with one or two legs off, some with their arms gone.

The *Kaiser* has been stuffing his men up that the English cannot shoot. They know differently now. They were greatly surprised when we picked them up and looked after them.

Pleased to say I am enjoying myself, and longing for more.

Letter 40.—From Gunner T. White:

We didn't waste more shots than was necessary on the Germans off Heligoland. One of their destroyers was knocked over first shot. It was one of the cleanest shots you ever saw, and the man who fired it is the proudest man in our ship to-day.

Next time I fancy the Germans will want to make it a rule of the fight that a German ship must be allowed at least ten shots to one of ours before the knock-out is fired. Of course, it's very hard on the rest of us, because it simply means that the gunner who gets first shot does the trick, and we may be in a dozen fights and never get a shot at the enemy once, because there's nothing left to hit.

Since that first engagement, the British Fleet has been waiting alert for the enemy to come out of hiding and give them a second chance; and has incidentally been busy sweeping the sea of floating mines and prowling after mine-layers that, disguised as Grimsby trawlers, have succeeded in putting in some deadly work.

An interesting account of the efficiency of this policing of the North Sea was related by two trawler skippers, a week after the fight, to a *Daily Telegraph* correspondent who remarks that the *modus operandi* necessitates a continuous vigilance, mostly under cover of the darkness, and entails a strain upon the naval officers and men that can only be appreciated by those who witness it.

The first skipper stated that he had just come from Iceland:

At one point up north there was, a solid wall of warships, which made it impossible for any foe to break through undetected. The scrutiny did not end with a mere examination at the point mentioned. After being released our boat was followed by a couple of torpedo destroyers until we reached our destination. In this way we were not only convoyed, but the warships made absolutely certain that we were British trawlers. The experience, being novel to us, was very inspiring.

The other skipper's story was even more interesting. He is in charge of a North Sea boat, and anchored each night near the shore.

We were laid under the land, he said, when about two in the morning a cruiser suddenly appeared alongside of us. All his lights were extinguished, and the quiet way in which he came up and the clever tactics he showed in getting alongside without doing any damage was astonishing.

Talk about cats seeing in the dark, these naval officers are wonderful. When the cruiser reached us all we could see was a huge black object hemming us in. A voice shouted out, "Who are you?" and I answered back, "A British trawler."

"What is your name?" he asked, and I replied.

"When did you leave?" he next asked. I told him.

"What were your orders when you left?" he next asked. I told him and in a flash the commander of the cruiser shouted back, "All right."

It was a fine piece of work, believe me, but there was something even more astonishing. Directly the commander had finished talking to me another voice from the stem of our vessel sung out, "The name is quite correct, sir." A submarine had crept up behind to verify our name and number, and although all the crew had come on deck to see what was happening, not one of the men aft had seen the submarine appear. The whole episode only occupied a few minutes, and the cruiser, after wishing us good morning and plenty of fishing, disappeared in the darkness. I have seen the British Navy in times of peace, but to see it in war time makes you feel proud of it. No swank, simply good old Nelson's motto all the time.

5

From Mons to the Walls of Paris

The Lilies of France and our own Red Rose
Are twined in a coronal now:
At War's bloody bridal it glitters and glows
On Liberty's beautiful brow.
Gerald Massey.

In his despatch to Lord Kitchener, dated September 7th, Sir John French tells of the four-days' battle at Mons, and traces his masterly, triumphant retreat, in the face of irresistible odds, to Maubeuge, to Cambrai, to Le Cateau, to Landrecies, and so almost to within sight of the walls of Paris. He pays a glowing tribute to the magnificent fighting spirit of the officers and men who carried out these stupendous movements with such complete success, but at present it is to the men themselves you must turn again for detailed information of the horrors and heroisms, the grim and glorious hours that darkened and lightened through those tumultuous days.

Private J. Harris, of the Worcestershire Regiment writes:

What we did in that three weeks English people at home will never know. We were marching and fighting day and night for three weeks without a break.

Letter 41.—From Private Smiley, of the Gordon Highlanders, to his brother, Mr. G. A . Smiley, of Chepstow:

On Sunday, 23rd, at Mons, we rose at four a.m. and marched out 1,100 strong. We took up ground on the extreme flank of the British force. Immediately we started to entrench ourselves, and to the good trench work we did we put down our freedom from casualty. Later in the day a hellish tornado of shell swept over us, and with this introduction to war we received our baptism of fire. We were lining the Mons road, and immediately in our front and to our rear were woods. In the rear wood was stationed a battery of R.F.A. The German artillery is wonderful. The first shot generally found us, and to me it looked as if the ranges had been carefully taken beforehand. However, our own gunners were better, and they hammered and battered the Germans all the day long.

They were at least three to our one, and our artillery could not be in fifty places at once, so we just had to stick it. The German infantry are bad skirmishers and rotten shots, and they were simply mowed down in batches by our chaps. They came in companies of, I should say, 150 men in file five deep, and we simply rained bullets at them the live-long day. At about five p.m. the Germans in the left front of us retired, and we saw no more of them.

The Royal Irish Regiment had had an awful smashing earlier on, as also had the Middlesex, and our company were ordered to go along the road as reinforcements. The one and a half mile seemed a thousand. Stormed at all the way, we kept on, and no one was hit until we came to a white house which stood in a clearing. Immediately the officer passed the gap hell was let loose on us, but we got across safely, and I was the only one wounded, and that was with a ricochet shrapnel bullet in the right knee.

I knew nothing about it until an hour after, when I had it pointed out to me. I dug it out with a knife. We passed dead civilians, some women, and a little boy with his thigh shattered by a bullet. Poor wee fellow. He lay all the time on his face, and some man of the Irish was looking after him, and trying to make him comfortable. The devils shelled the hospital and killed the wounded, despite a huge Red Cross flag flying over it.

When we got to the Royal Irish Regiment's trenches the scene was terrible. They were having dinner when the Germans opened on them, and their dead and wounded were lying all around. Beyond a go at some German cavalry, the day drew in, and darkness saw us on the retreat. The regiment lost one officer and one man dead, one officer and some men severely wounded.

We kept up this sort of game (fighting by day and retiring by night) until we got to Cambrai, on Tuesday night. I dare not mention that place and close my eyes. God, it was awful. Avalanche followed avalanche of fresh German troops, but the boys stuck to it, and we managed to retire to Ham without any molestation. Cambrai was the biggest battle fought. Out of all the glorious regiment of 1,100 men only five officers and 170 of the men answered the roll-call next day. Thank God, I was one of them.

Of course, there may be a number who got separated from the battalion through various causes, and some wounded who escaped. I hope so because of the heavy hearts at home. I saw the South Lancs, and they were terribly cut up, only a remnant left of the regiment.

Letter 42.—From Corporal W. Leonard, of the Army Service Corps (a South African War reservist) to his mother at Huddersfield:

I know that you will all excuse me for not receiving a letter from me this long time, but I hope that you will excuse me. Don't, whatever you do at home, don't worry about me. If I just thought that you won't worry at home I shall be all right. You know, mother, I know more about war this time than I did last, and the conditions also. It's all right when you know the ropes, and my African experiences are serving me in good stead here, so I hope and trust that you at home are not worrying about me; time enough to worry when there is cause. Well, I hope and trust all are well at home, as it is hell out here.

Up to this affair I thought that the Germans were a civilised race of people, but they are nothing but savages; niggers would not do what they do. Just fancy mounting maxim guns on ambulance wagons bearing the Red Cross, cutting the right hand off prisoners and turning them loose afterwards minus a hand. By jingo, mother, the boys (our boys) are absolutely all in. We did give the Boers a chance now and again, but these devils we don't give them a cat in hell chance; we're playing the game to the finish. I would not care to write so much, as I had better tell you when I come home. The Boer War was a tame affair.

We are moving off again tonight. I don't know where, and we don't care either; it's a do to a finish this time. I hope you got my postcards from Rouen in France, as there was some doubt as to whether they would let them through or not. I will write home as opportunity occurs, and I hope you won't worry about me, because you all know at home that I shall always be where I'm wanted, and my duty every time, so don't worry. Tell anyone who enquires I am O.K., lost a bit of weight perhaps, but not the worse so far, and above all don't believe all you see in the papers, as they know practically nothing, as everything is done under sealed orders, which never leak out. We are not even allowed to say in our letters where we are, as they are opened and read by the captain before they leave here, so you can judge for yourselves how things are. And I might say, mother, that we are very busy.

Letter 43.—From Corporal Edward Hood, to his father, at Taunton:

The fighting lately has been hot all round, and the French have had much harder than us in some places, but they're sticking at it manfully, and they deserve to win a victory that will wipe the Germans off the map. The French make a lot of us in camp, and when we pass each other in the field, no matter how busy the Frenchman may be, they give us hearty cheers to encourage us on our way. There's plenty of friendly rivalry between us when there's hard fighting to be done, and when we do get there before the French they don't grudge us our luck. They're good sports right through to the core, and the British soldier asks nothing better from allies in the field.

Letter 44,—From Private William Burgess, of the Royal Field Artillery, to his parents at Ilfracombe:

We left our landing place for the front, on the Tuesday, and got there on Saturday night. The Germans had just reached Liège then, and we got into action on the Sunday morning. The first thing we did was to blow up a bridge to stop the Germans from crossing. Then we came into action behind a lot of houses attached to the main street. We were there about ten minutes, when the houses started to fall around us. The poor people were buried alive. I saw poor children getting knocked down by bursting shells.

The next move was to advance across where there was a Red Cross Hospital. They dropped shells from airships and fired on it until the place was burnt down to the ground. Then they got a big plan on to retire and let the French get behind them. We retired eight miles, but we had to fight until we were forced to move again. We got as far as Le Cateau on Tuesday night. We camped there until two o'clock next morning.

Then we all heard there was a big fight coming off, so we all got together and cleared the field for action (The letter mentions the numbers of men engaged, and states that the Germans were in the proportion of three to one.) . . . We cut them down like rats. We could see them coming on us in heaps, and dropping like hail. The colonel passed along the line, and said, "Stick it, boys."

I tell you, mother, it was awful to see your own comrades dropping down—some getting their heads blown off, and others their legs and arms. I was fighting with my shirt off. A piece of shell went right through my shirt at the back and never touched me. It stuck into a bag of earth which we put between the wheels to stop bullets.

We were there all busy fighting when an airship came right over the line and dropped a bomb, which caused a terrible lot of smoke. Of course, that gave the Germans our range. Then the shells were dropping on us thick. We looked across the line and saw the German guns coming towards us. We turned our two centre guns on them, and sent them yards in the air. I reckon I saw one German go quite twenty yards in the air.

Just after that a shell burst right over our gun. That one got me out of action. I had to get off the field the best way I could. The bullets were going all around me on the way off; you see they got completely around us. I went about two miles, and met a Red Cross cart. I was taken to St. Quentin's Hospital. We were shelled out of there about two in the morning, and then taken in a train, and taken down to a plain near Rouen. Next morning we were put in a ship for dear old England.

Letter 45.—From a corporal in the King's Royal Rifles, now at Woolwich Hospital;

I was in three engagements, Mons, Landrecies, and Cambrai, but the worst of all was Mons. It was on Sunday, the 23rd of August, and I shall never forget the date. They were easily twenty-five to one, and we eventually had to retreat with just over a thousand casualties, but heavens, they must have had a jolly sight more. At Landrecies, where we arrived at 7.30, we thought we were going to have a night's rest, though we were wet through and no change, but we hadn't been there long before they (the Germans) started firing; they seemed to be in every place we went to. The only thing we heard then was, "turn out at once." It was about 10.15 when we turned out, and the colonel's orders were that we had to take a bridge if every man was killed. (I thought that sounded a wee bit healthy.) I had my last drink out of a dirty glass of beer. I says, "good health Billy," and off we went with bayonets fixed.

On our way to the bridge we met the regiment who had tried and failed, bringing back its wounded and killed in scores. (I thought more encouragement for the corps.) I was carrying my pal, the rifle, with my right hand. Well, we got near the bridge and found out from our scouts that there were 10,000 German troops on each side of the bridge and we were 1,300 strong. (More encouragement.) So we lined a long hedge about two yards apart so as to make a long line and harder for them to hit. We lay here till daybreak just before 4 a.m., and we could hear them talking all night about 300 yards away. We could see them quite clearly by this time; so we started to fire and rolled them over by dozens. It wasn't long, though, before the bullets were whizzing past my ears on each side, and I began to get my head lower and lower till I think I should have buried it in the mud if it had got much lower. Their superior numbers began to tell and we had to retire as fast as we could. I couldn't go fast enough with my pack on (it weighs 84 lbs.), so I threw it away as did hundreds more, and I finished bridge-taking with my old pal only (the rifle).

Letter 46.—From Lieutenant O. P, Edgcumbe, of 1st Battalion D.C.L.I., to his father, Sir Robert Edgcumbe, Commandant at Newquay .

29th August, 1914.

For the last week or ten days we have been fighting hard and are now for one day resting. Altogether, during five days and five nights, I got six hours' sleep, and so am rather weary. However, bullets and a real enemy are a wonderful stimulant, and I feel as fit as anything. Do all of you write as often as possible, and send me some newspapers. It does not matter whether there is any news—the sight of a letter from home is very cheering.

All our men are somewhat fatigued, but are very keen and full of fight. My regiment has had a bad time, and I am dreadfully afraid that they have been badly cut up, although I can as yet get no details. They were caught in a village by Germans in the houses, who had managed to get there by wearing our uniforms. Never again shall I respect the Germans, or any of them I may meet. They have no code of honour, and there have been several cases of their wearing French and British uniforms, which is, of course, against the Geneva Convention.

The weather is good, for which we are thankful.

Everything is so peaceful now, and it is such a perfect day that were it not for the continuous growl of the guns, which never cease, one would hardly believe one was in the midst of a huge war.

Letter 47.—From Private D. White:

German airships we seldom see now, though we used to have them every day over our heads. They are finding the French more than a match for them, and they most likely prefer to rely on their ordinary spies, of whom they have thousands. They are found often among the men engaged for transport work, but they are such clumsy bunglers that they give themselves away sooner or later. Some of us who haven't the heart to drown a cat never turn a hair when we see these scum shot, for they richly deserve what they get and a soldier's death is too good for them.

Letter 48.—From Private Spain, of the 4th Guards Brigade {late police-constable at Newry):

We have had three engagements with the Germans since I arrived, and I came out quite unhurt. The two first were fought on Sunday and Monday following. You see I cannot give date or place. Secrecy is our motto re war and movement of troops for international purposes, etc. Our third engagement was nearly fatal. We arrived at the town of ——, very much fatigued, and fully intending to have a good rest. It was a fine town, about as big as Newry, but more compact, with many fine buildings. We were just about five minutes billeted in the various houses, and just stretching our weary legs, when an officer came running in, shouting "The Germans are upon us; outside everyone."

We came out, magazine loaded, bayonets fixed, and eager to get a good bayonet fight with them. It appears they do not like it. But we found none. They had not yet arrived. It was 10 p.m. before they did so. In the meantime the poor people were leaving the town in crowds, with as much goods and chattels as they could carry away, and it was well for them, too. It was a dark night when we formed up in the streets, and the lamps but dimly burned. The noises of rifles and field guns were terrific. We rushed to the heads of the various streets, where our German foe would advance.

Our Field Artillery and the Coldstream Guards went out to delay their advance whilst we stripped off our coats and commenced to tear up the square setts, gather carts—in fact, everything that would build a barricade to keep back our numerous German foe, and we did so under perfect showers of shrapnel shell that struck and fell around us, and struck the houses about us, but we were undaunted, and so succeeded. Firing ceased, and we advanced out towards the Coldstream Guards' position. They had given them a good fight, but many of them lay for ever silent upon the ground. The Germans would not advance upon us, so we retired.

Letter 49. From Corporal Sam Moorhouse, of the King's Own Yorkshire Light Infantry, to his wife at Birkby:

Our company were reserves, and came under fire about noon. We were in a ditch as we thought safe when "*Ping! Ping!*" came the bullets, and off we shot across the open, under a railway embankment. On the way we passed four artillery horses shot dead with shrapnel. Then we took up a position on a hillside, when round the corner, 700 yards away, came a German maxim gun. They were busy getting it ready for firing on us, and we were firing at them, when our artillery which was only half a mile away sent two shots and blew up the gun and all the men. Then we cleared off and marched till twelve midnight. Up again at two and off for what was called a rest camp. Still wet clothes, and filthy ; had no boots off for days.

Instead of "rest" camp we marched nearly thirty miles, arriving at 8 p.m. Here I had a good meal of jam, cheese, and bread first bite of bread for days.

Next day we were up before daylight and taking up position. We dug trenches, and were fired on before we had finished. We were at the back a sort of last firing line. So we lay down in the trench, and waited. Shrapnel and lyddite were flying round us like hail, and our gunners were firing too. Such a noise! Just like thunder! Well, we stuck out as long as we could when we got the order to retire. However I came safely away goodness knows.

I picked up my gun and ran up the hill and dropped on one side of the road to rest. Then I had to get across the road, so got up and was half-way across when a shell burst and knocked me flat on my face. It must have fused at the wrong time, as I got only a cut on my thumb from a fragment. Then I got across and dropped in a trench where a fellow was lying dead. I stayed there only a minute, and then ran off over the hill and safe. The bullets were flying in all directions and shells were bursting four at a time. South Africa was nothing compared to this.

I had had no sleep for nights, so decided to go back to a little village we had just passed, where I sat on a doorstep till I fell asleep, and woke up one hour later wet through and chilled to the bone. It was still dark when I got back to where I left our regiment, and they were off. So I trekked away alone, and got on the wrong road.

About nine in the morning I came across some transport, and rode along with stragglers of other regiments to a camp. There were about sixty of us, and we went to a large camp, about 2,000 of us—all lost. There I came across Guy Jessop of Huddersfield, who was also lost, and was glad to meet a pal. We had a walk in the town together, and called in a *café*. We had some coffee and rum (Guy paid, as I had no money). I played the piano and sang "Mrs. Hullaby." Lucky job they could not understand English, or they would have been shocked.

Letter 50.—From Private E. W. Dyas, of the 11th Hussars, to his parents at Mountain Ash:

We landed at Havre, and travelled up country. We were under fire for about twenty minutes on the first day, and the shells were bursting like rain all around us. We got away with only one horse killed. It was marvellous. We are continually under

How the Royal Field Artillery Fight

fire by day and travelling by night. It is awful to hear the artillery booming death night and day. We were fighting day and night for three days. The slaughter was terrible. I took a dispatch across the battlefield when the Germans were retiring, and I passed their trenches. The dead were piled up in the trenches about ten deep, and there were trenches seven miles long. It was terrible to see. We are collecting the three cavalry brigades together at the present moment for a massive charge. I am writing this in the saddle. I may get through this again. One bullet penetrated my horse's neck and another one went through the saddle. I have had a sword-thrust through my sleeve. So I am getting on well.

Letter 51.—From Lieut. Oswald Anne, of the Royal Artillery, to his father. Major Anne, of Burghwallis Hall:

Dear Dad.—Just got yours of the 13th inst. Battling yesterday and the day before. I had a pal killed in another battery—five bullets in him. I have just seen the first Sausage-maker prisoner in hands of some infantry. They had the greatest difficulty in stopping the French populace from knifing him. The German shrapnel is very dangerous stuff, having high explosive in it. It bursts backwards, and so nullifies our frontal shield. No more time or news.

August 29th.

The boom of French guns is now in full swing, and we are standing easy for the moment. Did you get my other letter three days back? Just after I had finished it, we had the alarm, which proved false, but that night Germans marched into the town, thinking we had left it. So they say! A gruff German voice answered a challenge, and 15 rounds rapid fire from rifles and maxims behind the main road barricade, laid out every man. Eight hundred were picked up next morning in this one street.

An R.E. told me on the canal bridge a maxim fired 9,000 rounds and laid out another 1,000. The first Germans arriving in one end of this town were in French uniforms. Luckily, those in the rear were seen and fired on, stampeding the ammunition mules, scattering the "Sausages," who were almost laid out in a few rounds of fire. Lots of *"espions"* here, male and female. I have hardly seen a German, except prisoners. Poor Soames, of the 20th Hussars, was sparrowed first fight. W. Silvertop (20th Hussars) is hard at it "biffing" Sausages, and a N.C.O., yesterday, who had lost the regiment, told me 48 hours ago he was well. "Cigs." all arrived, and saved my life, also load of chocolate. Screaming women rush everywhere during conflicts howling *"Trahie,"* "Perdue," *"Sauve qui peut."* One of "D" battery, R.H.A.,N.C.O., told us they had mowed "Sausage-makers" down for ten minutes in one action as hard as they could load and still they came in masses, till at last the shrieking men ran all ways, not knowing where, leaving heaps of semi-moving remnants on the ground.

Our crowd, having so far escaped untouched, are very lucky. Several Brigades have had the devil's own hail of shot over them. Please send me some newspapers sometimes, as we have not seen one since I left, bar some old French *Petit Parisiens*.

The Scots Greys from York and the 12th Lancers did great work yesterday on hostile cavalry, and about wiped out those opposed to them. The "Guardies" are in great form. Very little sleep nowadays, up at dawn almost always, very often before that hour.

A German regiment, dressed in English uniforms, the other day billeted with an English regiment (at the other end of the town), and when the latter marched out they were about broken up by maxim fire from the bedroom windows. A German force arrived elsewhere, the Berkshire regiment were on guard, and the former, in French uniforms, called out from the wire entanglements that they waited to interview the C.O. A major went forward who spoke French, and was shot down immediately. This sort of thing is of daily occurrence, and only makes matters worse for the "Sausage-makers" when our infantry get into them.

Letter 52.—From a reservist in the Royal Field Artillery [Published in the *Glasgow Herald*):

I got a nasty hit with a shell on the thick of the leg. The Germans caught us napping on Wednesday, and what slaughter! It was horrible to witness. The Germans came along the village, killing the poor women and children and burning all the houses. Our division could not hold out. We were expecting the French troops to meet us, but they were two days late. Our battery had a lucky escape of being cut up. We entrenched our guns to come into action next day, but somehow or other we cleared out, and had only gone ten minutes before the place was blown up.

The officer in charge of my section had his head blown off. I was carried off under heavy fire on a fellow's back, and it is to him I owe my life. It was a long way to hospital, shells bursting all round us. We dropped behind some corn stacks, then on we went again. I had no sooner got bandaged up when a chap came galloping up and said the Germans were in sight. I was the second last man to leave the hospital, and ten minutes later it was blown up. You cannot imagine what things were like. The women and children of England can think themselves lucky, for the poor women here had to walk from village to village, young children in their arms. It touched my heart to see the sight. The Germans did not use rifles, but big guns, against our infantry's rifles. They are most brutal, killing all wounded in a most horrible fashion.

Letter 53.—From Trooper S. Cargill:

The Germans let all hell loose on us in their mad attempt to crush us and so win their way to Paris. They didn't succeed, and they won't succeed. I saw one ghastly affair. A German cavalry division was pursuing our retiring infantry when we were let loose on them. When they saw us coming they turned and fled, at least all but one, who came rushing at us with his lance at the charge. I caught hold of his horse, which was half mad with terror, and my chum was going to run the rider through when he noticed the awful glaze in his eyes and we saw that the poor devil was dead.

Letter 54.—From an Irish soldier, to his sister in County Cork:

I am writing this on a leaf out of a field service pocket-book, as notepaper and envelopes are very scarce, and we are not allowed to send picture postcards of places as they give away where we are. Well, this is a lovely country. The climate suits me very well. Everything grows like mad here. It is rather like Ireland, only ten times as rich. All that I have seen yet—and that is a good lot—is far and away better than the best part of the county Limerick. I think it would be a pleasure to farm here.

At the present time I am billeted in a farmhouse. I sleep in their best bed-room—that is when I can go to bed at all—and they give me home-made cider, cognac, and coffee, apples, plums, etc., and lovely home-made cheese for nothing, though they need not supply any food, as the rations are served out by the regiment every day.

'Tis great fun trying to talk French to them and I am picking it up gradually. It is wonderful how words and sentences that I learned at school come back to me now, and I can generally make myself understood all right. It is an awful pity to see this beautiful country spoiled by war, and it is no wonder the people are so eager to fight for it. I don't think there is a single house that has not sent out one or more men to fight with the French Army, and their mothers, sisters, wives, etc., are very proud of it. There are two gone out of this house.

Letter 55.—From Private Carwardine, to the father of a comrade-in-arms:

I am very sorry, but I don't know for sure about your Joe. You see, although he was in the same company as me, he was not in the same section. I only wish he had been. The last I saw of him was when we were in the firing line making trenches for ourselves. He was about 600 yards behind us, smoking, and I waved to him. Then all of a sudden we had to get down in our trenches, for bullets started coming over our heads, and shells dropped around us.

We were fighting twelve hours when I got one in the back from a shell. After that I knew no more until I found myself in hospital, and I asked one of our chaps how our company went on, and he told me there were only seventeen of us left out of 210. I hope Joe is among them. You will get to know in the papers in a bit when they call the roll.

So cheer up and don't be downhearted, for if Joe is killed he has died a soldier of honour on the field. Excuse writing, as I am a bit shaky, and I hope to God Joe is safe, for both your sakes.

Letter 56.—From Private G. Dunton, of the Royal Engineers, to his family at Coventry :.

I am in hospital, having been sent home from France, wounded in my left hand. I have got one shrapnel bullet right through my hand, and another through my middle finger against the top joint. I was wounded at Cambrai last Wednesday. I have been in four hospitals in France, but had to be removed on account of the Germans firing on the hospitals. I do not think much of them, for if it was not for their artillery they would be wiped out in quick time. No doubt our losses are great, but theirs are far more.

The famous cavalry of theirs, the Uhlans, are getting cut up terribly. All that have been captured have said that they are short of food. I must say we have had plenty to eat. I was near Mons a week last Saturday and we were attacked the same day. We have been on the retire ever since last Wednesday, when I got wounded, but we shall soon be advancing, for they will never reach Paris. I am very pleased to see that the Germans are being forced back by the Russians. I hope they will serve Berlin the same as the Germans have done to Belgium. The 9th Brigade was cut up badly; in fact, my division was, but more are wounded than killed.

There are 1,000 wounded in this hospital alone, without other hospitals. I must say that I am in good health. My hand is giving me pain, but I do not mind that. I only had four days' fighting, but it was hard work while it lasted. The Germans, although four to one, could not break through our lines, and they must have lost thousands, as our artillery and infantry mowed them down like sheep. Their rifle fire took no effect at all. All our wounds were done by shrapnel. My hand is not healing at all, but I must be patient and give it time. The French and Belgian people were very kind to us and gave us anything we wanted.

Letter 57.—From a Manchester soldiery in a French hospital:

There was a young French girl helping to bandage us up. How she stood it I don't know. There were some awful sights, but she never quailed—just a sweet, sad smile for everyone. If ever anyone deserved a front seat in Heaven, this young angel does. God bless her. She has the prayers and the love of the remnants of our division. All the French people are wonderfully generous. They gave us anything and everything. You simply cannot help loving them, especially the children.

Letter 58.—From Private A. McGillivray, a Highlander, to his mother:

Of my company only 10 were unhit. I saw a handful of Irishmen throw themselves in front of a regiment of cavalry who were trying to cut off a battery of horse artillery. It was one of the finest deeds I ever saw. Not one of the poor lads got away alive, but they made the German devils pay in kind, and, anyhow, the artillery got away to account for many more Germans. Every man of us made a vow to avenge the fallen Irishmen, and if the German cavalrymen concerned were made the targets of every British rifleman and gunner they had themselves to thank. Later they were fully avenged by their own comrades, who lay in wait for the German cavalrymen. The Irish lads went at them with the bayonet when they least expected it, and the Germans were a sorry sight. Some of them howled for mercy, but I don't think they got it. In war mercy is only for the merciful.

Letter 59.—From Private W. Bell, of the 2nd South Lancashire Regiment to his wife:

I shall never forget this lot. Men fell dead just like sheep. Our regiment was first in the firing line, and we were simply cut up. Very few escaped, so I think I was very lucky, for I was nearly half-a-mile creeping over nothing but dead men. In the trenches, bullets and shells came down on us like rain. We even had to lift dead men up and get under them for safety.
When we got the order to retire an officer was just giving the order to charge when he was struck dead, and it is a good job we didn't charge, or we would have all been killed. I passed a lot of my chums dead, but I didn't see Fred Atkinson (a friend of the family).

Letter 60.—From Corporal T. Trainor;

Have you ever seen a little man fighting a great, big, hulking giant who keeps on forcing the little chap about the place until the giant tires himself out, and then the little one, who has kept his wind, knocks him over? That's how the fighting round here strikes me. We are dancing about round the big German army, but our turn will come.
Last Sunday we had prayers with shells bursting all around us,

but the service was finished before it was necessary for us to grapple with the enemy. The only thing objectionable I have seen is the robbing of our dead and wounded by German ghouls. In such cases no quarter is given, and, indeed, is never expected.

Letter 61.—From an artilleryman, to his wife at Sheerness:

I am the only one left out of my battery; we were blown to pieces by the enemy on Wednesday at Le Cateau. We have been out here twenty-eight days all told, and have been through the five engagements. I have nothing; only the jacket I stand up in—no boots or putties, as I was left for dead. But my horse was shot, and not me. He laid down on me. They had to cut my boots, etc., off to get me from under my horse.

Letter 62.—From Lance-Corporal J. Preston, of the 2nd Battalion Inniskilling Fusiliers, to his wife at Banbridge;

I did not get hit at Mons. I got through it all right. We encountered the Germans on Sunday at Mons, and fought on till Monday night. It was on the retreat from Mons that I was caught. They had about one hundred guns playing on us all the time we were retiring. We had a battery of artillery with us. They were all blown to pieces, men and guns and all. It was a most sorrowful sight to see the guns wiped out, and the gunners and men lying around them. The whole plain was strewn with dead and wounded. I hope my eyes will never look on anything so horrid again. Our section brought in six prisoners, all wounded, and they told us we had slain hundreds of them. We captured a German spy; he was dressed in a Scotsman's uniform, and was knocking around our camp, but we were a bit too quick for him. I think the hardest battles are fought; the German cannot stand it much longer, his food supply is getting done.

Letter 63.—From a corporal in the Motor Cycle Section of the Royal Engineers:

Last night the enemy made an attempt to get through to our base in armed motors. Myself and two other motorcyclists were sent out to look for them. It was a pitch-black night, with a thick fog. One of our men got in touch with them, and was pursued. He made for a bridge which had been mined by the engineers, and that was the end of the Germans. . . . The German artillery is rotten. Last Saturday three batteries bombarded an entrenched British battalion for two hours, and only seven men were killed. The noise was simply deafening, but so little effect had the fire that the men shouted with laughter, and held their caps up on the end of their rifles to give the German gunners a bit of encouragement.

This is really the best summer holiday I have had for a long time.

Letter 64.—From Corporal J. Bailey:

It's very jolly in camp in spite of all the drawbacks of active service, and we have lively times when the Germans aren't hanging around to pay their respects. It's a fine sight to see us on the march, swinging along the roads as happy as schoolboys, and singing all the old songs we can think of. The tunes are sometimes a bit out, but nobody minds so long as we're happy. As we pass through the villages the French come out to cheer us and bring us food and fruit. Cigarettes we get more of than we know what to do with. Some of them are rotten, so we save them for the German prisoners, who would smoke anything they can lay their hands on. Flowers also we get plenty of, and we are having the time of our lives.

Letter 65.—From a sergeant in the Royal Field Artillery:

If the French people were mad about us before we were on trial, they are absolutely crazy over us now when we have sort of justified our existence. In the towns we pass through we are received with so much demonstration that I fancy the French soldiers must be jealous. The people don't seem to have eyes for anybody but us, and they do all they can to make us comfortable. They give us the best they can lay hold of, but that's not much after the Germans have been around collaring all they could. It's the spirit that means so much to us, and even though it was only an odd cup of water they brought us we would be grateful. Most of us are glad to feel that we are fighting for a nation worth fighting for, and after our experience there can be no question of trouble between us and France in the future.

We lost terribly in the retreat from Mons, of which you have heard by now, but artillery always stands to lose in retreats, because we play such a big part in getting the other men away and we quite made up our minds that we would have to pay forfeit then. Without boasting, I can say that it was the way the guns were handled that made it so easy for our lads to get out of the German trap.

There was once or twice when it looked as though it were all up with us, and some of our chaps were fair down in the mouth over it; but I think now they didn't make sufficient allowance for the steadiness of all arms of our service; and, between ourselves, I think they had got the usual notions about the splendid soldiering qualities of the German army. They know better now, and though it's bad to get chesty about that sort of thing, we are all pretty confident that with a sporting chance we stand to win all the time.

Letter 66.—From Private J. Toal:

It's tired we all were when we got through that week of fighting and marching from Mons; but after we'd had a taste of rest for a day or two, by the saints, we were ready for the ugly Germans again, and we've been busy ever since drilling holes in them big enough to let out the bad that's in them. You wouldn't believe the way they have burned and destroyed the holy churches everywhere they went, and there's many an Irish lad betwixt here and the frontier has registered a vow that he will not rest content till he's paid off that score against the men who would lay hands on God's altars.

Letter 67.—From Private W. Green;

We see more Germans than you could count in the day, but they are now very funky about it, and they will never wait for a personal interview with one of our men, especially if he has a lance or a bayonet handy, and naturally you don't go out German-hunting without something of the kind with you, if only just for luck. When they must face us they usually get stuck away somewhere where they are protected by more guns than you ever set eyes on, and likewise crowds of machine guns of the Maxim pattern, mounted on motors. These are not now so troublesome, for they are easy to spot out in the open, and our marksmen quickly pick off the men serving them, so the Germans are getting a bit shy about displaying them. Something we heard the other day has put new life into us; not that we were downhearted before, but what I mean shows that we are going to have all we wished for very soon, and though we can't tell you more you may be sure that we are going on well.

Letter 68.—From Private G, A. Turner, to his father, Mr. J. W, Turner, of Leeds (Published in the *Leeds Mercury*):

I am still living, though a bit knocked about.

I got a birthday present from the *Kaiser*. I was wounded on the 23rd. So it was a near thing, was it not? I got your letter at a place called Moroilles, in France, about five miles from Landrecies, where our troops have retired.

On Sunday, 23rd, we had rifle inspection at 11 a.m., and were ordered to fall in for bathing parade at 11.30. While we were waiting for another company to return from the river the Germans commenced to shell the town. We fell in about 1.0 p.m., an hour and a half afterwards, to go to the scene of the attack. Shells were bursting in the streets as we went. We crossed a bridge over the canal under artillery fire, and stood doing nothing behind a mill on the bank for some time.

Then someone cried out that the Germans were advancing along the canal bank, and our company were ordered to go along. We thought we were going to check the Germans, but we found out afterwards that a company of our own regiment were in position further along on the opposite side of the canal, and we were being sent out to reinforce them.

There was no means of crossing the canal at that point, so it was an impossibility. As soon as we started to move we were spotted by the Germans, who opened fire with their guns at about five hundred yards with shrapnel, and the scene that followed beggars description. Several of us were laid full length behind a wooden fence about half an inch thick. The German shells burst about three yards in front of it. It was blown to splinters in about ten minutes. None of us expected to get out alive.

They kept us there about an hour before they gave us the word to retire. I had just turned round to go back when I stopped one. It hits you with an awful thump, and I thought it had caught me at the bottom of the spine, as it numbed my legs for about half an hour.

When I found I could not walk I gave it up. Just after, I got my first view of the Germans. They were coming out of a wood about 400 yards away all in a heap together, so I thought as I was done for I would get a bit of my own back, and I started pumping a bit of lead into them.

I stuck there for about three-quarters of an hour, and fired all my own ammunition and a lot belonging to two more wounded men who were close to me—about 300 rounds altogether, and as it was such a good target I guess I accounted for a good lot of them.

Then I suddenly discovered I could walk, and so I set off to get back. I had to walk about 150 yards in the open, with shrapnel bursting around me all the way, but somehow or other I got back without catching another. It was more than I expected, I can assure you, and I laughed when I got in the shelter of the mill again.

I was very sorry to have to leave the other chaps who were wounded, but as I could only just limp along I could not help them in any way. They were brought in later by stretcher bearers.

A man who was at Paardeburg and Magersfontein, in South Africa, said they were nothing to what we got that Sunday. Out of 240 men of my company only about twenty were uninjured.

Letter 69.—From an infantryman in hospital (Published in the *Aldershot News*);

I found myself mixed up with a French regiment on the right. I wanted to go forward with them, but the officer in charge shook his head and smiled, "They will spot you in your khaki and put you out in no time," he said in English; "make your way to the left; you'll find your fellows on that hill." I watched the regiment till it disappeared; then I made my way across a field and up a big avenue of trees. The shells were whistling overhead, but there was nothing to be afraid of. Halfway up the avenue there was a German lancer officer lying dead by the side of the road. How he got there was a mystery, because we had seen no cavalry. But there he lay, and someone had crossed his hands on his breast, and put a little celluloid crucifix in his hands. Over his face was a beautiful little handkerchief—a lady's—with lace edging. It was a bit of a mystery, because there wasn't a lady for miles that I knew of.

Letter 70.—From Sapper H. Mugridge, R.E., to his mother at Uckfleld:

We met the Germans at Landrecies on Sunday. We had a fifteen-hour battle. It was terrible. There were 120,000 Germans and only 20,000 of us, but our men fought well. We blew up six bridges. Laid our charges in the afternoon, and the whole time we were doing it were not hit. After we had got everything ready we got back into cover and waited until 1.30 on Monday morning, until our troops had got back over the river, and then we blew up the bridges. We retired about thirty miles. The town where we stopped on Sunday was a beautiful place, but the Germans destroyed it. Close to where I was a church had been used as a hospital, and our wounded were coming by the dozens. But, terrible to say, the Germans blew the place up. They have no pity. They kill our wounded and drive the people before them.

Letter 71.—From Sapper H. Mugridge, R.E. (Second letter, published in the *Sussex Daily News*):

We were laying our gun cotton—ten of us were the last to leave, and the Germans stopped us. We had to run for it down the main street of the town of Landrecies, and, being dark, we could not see where we were going. We got caught in some telegraph wires which had been put across the street. We had to cut them away with our bayonets. On Monday morning, when things were quieter, we went nearly into the German lines. We could hear them giving orders. Our job was to put barbed wire across the road. I was thankful to get out of it. We could see the Germans burning their dead. They must have lost a few thousand men, as our troops simply mowed them down. I saw one sergeant kill fourteen Germans, one after the other. They came up in fifties, all in a cluster, and you couldn't help hitting them. They were only 400 yards from us all day on Sunday. They are very cruel. Our people used a church for a hospital, and it was filled with our wounded, but the place was shelled and knocked down. They stabbed a good many of our men while lying on the battlefield. They have no respect for the Red Cross. To see women and children driven from home and walking the roads is terrible—old men and women just the same.

At the town where we were we got cut off from our people—eighteen of us—and the houses were being toppled over by the German artillery. The people clung around us, asking us to stay with them, but it was no good. When we left, the town was in flames. But our men did fight well. You never saw anything so cool in your life. Anyone would have thought it was a football match, for they were joking and laughing with one another.

Letter 72—From John Baker, of the Royal Flying Corps, to his parents at Boston, Lincolnshire:

While flying over Boulogne at a height of 3,000 feet, something went wrong with the machine, and the engine stopped. The officer said, "Baker, our time has come. Be brave, and die like a man. Goodbye," and shook hands with me. I shall always remember the ten minutes that followed. The next I remembered was that I was in a barn. I was removed to Boulogne, and afterwards to Netheravon, being conveyed from Southampton by motor ambulance.

Letter 73.—From Private G. Rider:

The Germans are good and bad as fighters, but mostly bad so far as I have seen. They are nearly all long distance champions in the fighting line, and won't come too near unless they are made to. Yesterday we had a whole day of it in the trenches, with the Germans firing away at us all the time. It began just after breakfast, and we were without food of any kind until we had what you might call a dainty afternoon tea in the trenches under shell fire. The mugs were passed round with the biscuits and the "bully" as best they could by the mess orderlies, but it was hard work getting through without getting more than we wanted of lead rations.

My next-door neighbour, so to speak, got a shrapnel bullet in his tin mug, and another two doors off had his biscuit shot out of his hand when he was fool enough to hold it up to show it to a chum in the next trench.

We are ready for anything that comes our way, and nothing would please us better than a good big stand-up fight with the Germans on any ground they please. We are all getting used to the hard work of active service, and you very seldom hear complaints from anybody. The grousers, who are to be found in nearly every regiment, seem to be on holiday for the war.

Letter 74.—From Private Martin O'Keefe, of the Royal Irish Rifles, to his friends at Belfast:

Our part in the fighting was limited almost entirely to covering the retreat by a steady rifle fire from hastily-prepared trenches. We were thrown out along an extended front, and instructed to hold our ground until the retiring troops were signalled safe in the next position allotted them. When this was done our turn came, and we retired to a new position, our place being taken by the light cavalry, who kept the Germans in check as long as they could and then fell back in their turn. The Germans made some rather tricky moves in the hope of cutting us off while we were on this dangerous duty, but our flanks were protected by cavalry, French and English, and they did not get very far without having to fight.

When they found the slightest show of resistance they retreated, and tried to find an easier way of getting in at us. The staff were well pleased with the way we carried out the duty given to us, and we were told that it had saved our army from very serious loss at one critical point. We put in some wonderfully effective shooting in the trenches, and the men find it is much easier making good hits on active service than at manoeuvres. The Germans seemed to think at first that we were as poor shots as they are, and they were awfully sick when they had to face our deadly fire for the first time.

Letter 75.—From Sergeant W. Holmes:

We are off again, this time with some of the French, and it's enough to give you fits to hear the Frenchmen trying to pick up the words of "Cheer Boys, Cheer," which we sing with great go on the march. They haven't any notion of what the words mean, but they can tell from our manner that they mean we're in good heart, and that's infectious here. We lost our colonel and four other officers in our fight on Tuesday. It was the hottest thing we were ever in. The colonel was struck down when he was giving us the last word of advice before we threw ourselves on the enemy. We avenged him in fine style. His loss was a great blow to us, for he was very popular.

It's always the best officers, somehow, that get hit the first, and there's not a man in the regiment who wouldn't have given his life for him. He was keen on discipline, but soldiers don't think any less of officers who are that. The German officers are a rum lot. They don't seem in too great a hurry to expose their precious carcasses, and so they "lead" from the rear all the time. We see to it that they don't benefit much by that, you may be sure, and when it's at all possible we shoot at the skulking officers. That probably accounts for the high death rate among German officers. They seem terribly keen on pushing their men forward into posts of danger, but they are not so keen in leading the way, except in retreat, when they are well to the fore. Our cavalry are up to that little dodge, and so, when they are riding out to intercept retreating Germans, they always give special attention to the officers.

Letter 76.—From Corporal J. Hammersley:

The Germans in front of us are about done for, and that's the truth of it. They have got about as much fighting as humans can stand, and it is about time they realised it. I don't agree with those who think this war is going to last for a long time. The pace we go at on both sides is too hot, and flesh and blood won't stand it for long. My impression is that there will be a sudden collapse of the Germans that will astonish everybody at home; but we are not leaving much to chance, and we do all we can to hasten the collapse. The Germans aren't really cut out for this sort of work. They are proper bullies, who get on finely when everybody's lying bleeding at their feet, but they can't manage at all when they have to stand up to men who can give them more than they bargain for.

Letter 77.—From Lance-Corporal T. Williams:

We are now getting into our stride and beginning to get a little of our own back out of the Germans. They don't like it at all now that we are nearer to them in numbers, and their men all look like so many "Weary Willies;" they are so tired. You might say they have got "that tired feeling" bad, and so they have. Some of them just drop into our arms when we call on them to surrender as though it were the thing they'd been waiting for all their lives.

One chap who knows a little English told us he was never more pleased to see the English uniform in all his life before, for he was about fed up with marching and fighting in the inhuman way the German officers expect their men to go on. When we took him to camp he lay down and slept like a log for hours; he was so done up.

That's typical of the Germans now, and it looks as though the *Kaiser* were going to have to pay a big price for taxing his men so terribly. You can't help being sorry for the poor fellows. They all say they were told when setting out that it would be child's play beating us, as our army was the poorest stuff in the world. Those who had had experience in England didn't take that in altogether, but the country yokels and those who had never been outside their own towns believed it until they had a taste of our fighting quality, and then they laughed with the other side of their faces.

That's the Germans all over, to "kid" themselves into the belief that they have got a soft thing, and then when they find it's too hard, to run away from it. Our lads have made up their minds to give them no rest once we get on to them, and they'll get as much of the British Army as they can stand, and maybe a little more. The French are greatly pleased with the show we made in the field, and are in much better spirits than they were.

Letter 78.—From a non-commissioned officer of dragoons:

All our men—in fact, the whole British Army—are as fit as a fiddle, and the lads are as keen as mustard. There is no holding them back. At Mons we were under General Chetwode, and horses and men positively flew at the Germans, cutting through much heavier mounts and heavier men than ours. The yelling and the dash of the lancers and Dragoon Guards was a thing never to be forgotten. We lost very heavily at Mons, and it is a marvel how some of our fellows pulled through and positively frightened the enemy. We did some terrible execution, and our wrists were feeling the strain of heavy riding before sunset. With our tunics unbuttoned, we had the full use of our right arm for attack and defence.

After Mons I went with a small party scouting, and we again engaged about twenty cavalry, cut off from their main body. We killed nine, wounded six, and gave chase to the remaining five, who, in rejoining their unit, nearly were the means of trapping us. However, our men dispersed and hid in a wood until they fell in with a squadron of the ———, and so reached camp in safety. After that a smart young corporal accompanied me to reconnoitre, and we went too far ahead, and were cut off in a part of the country thick with Uhlans. As we rode in the direction of ——— two wounded men were limping along, both with legs damaged, one from the Middlesex and the other Lancashire Fusiliers, and so we took them up.

Corporal Watherston took one behind his saddle and I took the other. The men were hungry, and tattered to shreds with fighting, but in fine spirits. We soon came across a small village, and I found the *curé* a grand sportsman and full of pluck and hospitality. He seemed charmed to find a friend who was English, and told me that the Germans were dressed in the uniforms of British soldiers, which they took from the dead and from prisoners in order to deceive French villagers, who in many places in that district had welcomed these wolves in sheep's clothing. We were warned that the enemy would be sure to track us up to the village.

The *curé* said he could hide the two wounded men in the crypt of his church and put up beds for them. It has a secret trapdoor, and was an ancient treasure-house of a feudal lord, whose castle we saw in ruins at the top of the hill close by. Then he hid away our saddlery and uniforms in the roof of a barn, and insisted upon our making a rest-chamber of the tower of his church, which was approached by a ladder, which we were to pull up to the belfry as soon as we got there. He smuggled in wine and meat and bread and cakes, fruit and cigarettes, with plenty of bedding pulled up by a rope. We slept soundly, and the owls seemed the only other tenants, who resented our intrusion. No troops passed through the village that night. In the morning the *curé* came round at six o'clock, and we heard him say Mass. After that we let down the ladder, and he came up with delicious hot chocolate and a basket of rolls and butter.

Our horses he had placed in different stables a mile apart, and put French "fittings "on them, so as to deceive the enemy. He thinks we are well away from the main body of the German Army moving in the direction of Paris, but will not hear of our leaving here for at least three days. But I cried, "*Curé*, we are deserters!" The old man wept and said, "Deserters, no, no—

saviours, saviours; you have rescued France from the torments of slavery."

However, we have now secured complete disguises as French *cultivateurs*—baggy corduroy trousers, blue shirts, boots, stockings, belt, hat, cravat, everything to match—and as we have not shaved for two weeks, and are bronzed with the sun, I think that the corporal and myself can pass anywhere as French peasants, if only he will leave all the talking to me.

The two wounded soldiers don't wish us to leave them, because I am interpreter, and not a soul speaks English in the village. So we have explained to the *curé* that we shall stay here until our comrades are able to walk, and then the party of four will push our way out somewhere on horseback and get to the coast. The sacristan at once offered to be our guide, and it is arranged that we take a carrier's wagon which travels in this district and drive our own horses in it, and pick up two additional mounts at a larger village on the way to the coast.

We must get back as soon as ever we can. Nothing could be kinder than the people here, but this is not what we came to France for, and hanging about in a French village is not exactly what a soldier calls "cricket."

You cannot imagine how complete the Germans are in the matter of rapid transport. Large automobiles, such as the railway companies have for towns round Harrogate and Scarborough, built like *char-a-bancs,* carry the soldiers in batches of fifty, so that they are as fresh as paint when they get to the front. But in point of numbers I think one of our side is a fair match for four of the enemy.

I hope that the British public are beginning to understand what this war means. The German is not a toy terrier, but a bloodhound absolutely thirsty for blood.

Letter 79.—From Private Tom Savage, to his relatives at Larne:

At Sea.

Just a line to let you know that we are landing outside ——. They kept us without any knowledge of how and where we were going till the last moment. I am quite well and extra specially fit. It is good fun on a troopship, and we are going to have a nice little holiday on the Continent. I'll be able to "swank French" when I come back. I'll write a good long letter when

I settle down. I'm writing this at tea time just before we land. I have got two very nice chums, Jack Wright, the footballer, who has seen service before, and Billy Caughey, both of Belfast.

In France.

I am writing this note while on outpost duty. I can't say where we are, or anything like that, but I am in the best of health and enjoying the life. I am getting a fine hand at French. There is plenty of food and the people are all very nice. It's great fun trying to understand them. Plenty of fruit here, pears and apples galore, and as for bread big long rolls and rings of it, and all very cheap. When you happen to be riding through a town the people give you cigarettes, fruit, chocolates, and cider.

If you are all extra good I'll bring you home a pet German. How is Home Rule getting on? Send me a paper, but I don't know when I'll get it or you'll get this. I suppose the papers are full of this ruction. I can write no more as I'll soon have to go on guard.

Letter 80.—From Mons. E. Hovelange, of Paris, written on August 30th, to Sir William Collins (Published in the *Sussex Daily News*):

How serious the situation is here it is hard for you to realize in London. We may be encircled at any moment by these hordes of savages. Such murderous cruelty has never been seen in the annals of war. The Turks and the Bulgarians were no worse. It is the rule to fire on ambulances and slaughter the wounded. I know it from eyewitnesses. The Germans are drunk with savagery. It is an orgy of the basest cruelty. They are rushing Paris at all costs, squandering their men recklessly in overwhelming numbers.

Our troops are submerged and can only retreat, fighting desperately, but the spirit of our soldiers is splendid. All the wounded I have seen laugh and joke over their wounds and are burning to have another go at the barbarians. Victory is certain. But what disastrous changes shall we know before it comes. I am prepared for the worst—another month of hopeless struggle perhaps. But we will fight to the last man. The tide will turn, and then— woe to them. I know you will stand by us in the cause of civilization, common honest truth till the bitter end. But if you want to help us you must hasten.

Letter 81.—From a young officer who has been through the whole campaign, from the landing of the British at Boulogne:

I wish you would try to make the people in England understand that they should be most exceedingly thankful that they are living on an island and not in the midst of the dreadful things which are happening on the Continent. Do enforce upon the public that England must fight this thing out, and must conquer even if it has to spend the blood of its young men like water. It will be far better that every family throughout England should have to sorrow for one of its members than that England should have to go through similar ordeals to those which Continental countries are suffering.

The sight of old women and men fleeing from village to village; young mothers with babies in arms, with their few personal effects on their backs, or in some more fortunate cases with their goods and chattels surrounding the aged grandmother stowed away in an old farm cart, drawn by a nag too venerable to be of service to the State; this is what one has seen daily. Picture to yourself our night marches with the burning villages on all sides set fire to by German shells—and the Germans have been rather careless whether their shells struck fortified and defended positions, or open ones. In some cases the fires were caused intentionally by marauding patrols.

Do not imagine that things are not going well with us. We are all satisfied and confident of the end; but at the same time the only possible end can be gained by sacrifice on the part of those at home only. All is well with me personally; I have a busy time, but it is most interesting work.

In Hospital.

(1) At Salisbury.

A non-commissioned officer of the Royal Field Artillery, invalided home with shrapnel wounds in the thigh, from which he hopes soon to recover, has given this vivid description of his experiences at the front after passing north of Amiens, to a *Daily Telegraph* correspondent:

"Pushing forward from our rest camp, covering from twenty to thirty miles a day, with the infantry marching in front and cavalry protecting us on either flank, we received information that we were within a few hours' march of the enemy. Needless to say, this put us on the alert. There was no funk about us, for we were all anxious to have a go at the Germans, about whom we had heard such tales of cruelty that it made our blood run cold.

Our orders were to load with case shot, for fear of cavalry attack, as shrapnel is of little use against mounted troops. The order was soon obeyed, and after passing the day on the road, we moved across country north of ——, where the infantry took up a strong position. We saw the French troops on our right as we moved up to gun positions which our battery commanders had selected in advance. It was Sunday morning when the attack came, and the sun had already lit up the beautiful country, and as I looked across at the villages which lay below in the valley with their silent belfries I thought of my home on the Cotswolds and of the bells ringing for morning service. I pictured dad and my sister Nell going to church.

"It was, however, no time for sentiment, for gallopers soon brought the news that the enemy was advancing, and that a cavalry attack might be expected at any moment. Infantry had entrenched themselves along our front, and there was a strong body posted on our flanks and rear. These became engaged first with a large body of Uhlans, who endeavoured to take them by surprise, the front rank rushing forward with the lance and the rear using the sword.

We were on slightly higher ground, and could see the combat, which appeared to be going in our favour. Our men stuck to their ground and shot and bayoneted the Uhlans, who, after ten minutes' fight, made off, but, sad to say, a dreadful fusillade of shrapnel and Maxim fire followed immediately, and our guns also came under fire. To this we readily replied, and must have done some execution, especially to the large masses of infantry that were advancing about a mile away.

We got a favourable "bracket" at once, so our major said, and we worked our guns for all we were worth, altering fuses and the ranging of our guns as the Germans came nearer. Shells fell fast around us, some ricocheted, and passed overhead without bursting, ploughing the ground up in our rear, but not a few exploded, and made many casualties. Three of my gun detachment fell with shrapnel bullets, but still we kept the guns going, the officers giving a hand.

At one time we came under the fire of the enemy's machine guns, but two of our 18-pounders put them out of action after a few rounds. The order came at length to retire so as to get a more favourable position, but our drivers failed to bring back all the gun teams, only sufficient to horse four of the guns. The remainder of the animals had been terribly mutilated. These were limbered up, the remainder being for a time protected by the infantry. The Gordons and Middlesex were in the shelter trenches on our left, and the latter regiment was said at one time to be almost overwhelmed, but aid came, and the masses of Prussian infantry were beaten off.

Still, there was terrible slaughter on both sides, and the dead lay in long burrows on the turf. We should have lost our guns to the Uhlans if the infantry had not persevered with the rifle, picking off the cavalry at 800 yards.

It was grand shooting. In the afternoon we slackened fire, as also did the Germans; in fact, we did but little from our new gun positions, as we were destined to cover the retreat of the infantry later on.

As the wounded were brought to the rear we heard of the deeds of heroism from the men of the Royal Army Medical Corps in the fighting line—how an officer stood over the body of a private who had previously saved his life until he had spent his last shot from his revolver, and then fell seriously wounded, to be avenged the next moment by a burly sergeant who plunged his bayonet into the Prussian.

In the ranks of the South Lancashire Regiment, from what has been heard, many deserve the Distinguished Conduct Medal, if not the V.C., for the manner in which they charged masses of German infantry through the village to our front. Uhlans got round behind them, but they did not flinch, although serious gaps were made in their ranks.

A non-commissioned officer of the Medicals related how he saw a party of Fusiliers rush to the aid of their Maxim gun party when Uhlans swept down on them from behind a wood. They accounted for over twenty and lost but one man.

At night we were ordered to move on again and we marched south-west in the direction of ——, covering twenty miles in the darkness. Our unhorsed guns were got through by splitting up our teams, and with the help of the brawny arms of the infantry. . The enemy were aware of our retreat, and kept up an incessant fire, bringing searchlights to the aid of their gunners. The moon slightly favoured us, and, with the help of local guides, we found our way. I heard of the brilliant work performed by our battalions, who kept the enemy at bay whilst we withdrew all our vehicles, and we gunners felt proud of them. They kept the enemy busy by counter-attack, and made it impossible to get round us.

Next morning the enemy were again in the field endeavouring to force our left flank. Field-Marshal Sir John French, whom we saw early in the day, was, however, equal to the occasion, and so manoeuvred his troops that we occupied a position from which the Germans could not dislodge us. The artillery kept up long-range fire, and that is how I received my wound. Within a few minutes first aid was rendered, and I was put in an ambulance and taken off with other wounded to a field hospital, where I met with every attention.

(2) At the London Hospital. By a *Daily Telegraph* correspondent.

A description of a thrilling fight in the air, which had a dramatic climax, was given to Queen Alexandra when Her Majesty paid a visit to the London Hospital.

Among the wounded soldiers there is a private of the Royal Engineers, who was himself witness of the incident.

He said that following a very hard fight on the day before, he was lying on the ground with his regiment, resting.

"Suddenly a German aeroplane hove in sight. It flew right over the British troops, and commenced to signal their position to the German camp.

A minute later, amid intense excitement of the troops, two aeroplanes, with English and French pilots, rose into the air from the British rear. Ascending with great rapidity, they made for the German aeroplane, with the intention of attacking it.

At first some of our men, who were very much on the alert, fired by mistake at the French aeroplane. Luckily, their shots went wide.

Then the troops lay still, and with breathless interest watched the attempts of the French and British aviators to outmanoeuvre their opponent, and to cut off his retreat. After a little time the Franco-British airmen abandoned this attempt, and then the Englishman and the German began to fly upwards, in the evident desire to obtain a more favourable position for shooting down from above. Owing to the protection afforded by the machine, it would have been of little use for one aviator to fire at his opponent from below. Once a higher altitude was attained, the opportunity for effective aim would be much greater.

Up and up circled the two airmen, till their machines could barely be distinguished from the ground. They were almost out of sight when the soldiers saw that the British aviator was above his opponent. Then the faint sound of a shot came down from the sky, and instantly the German aeroplane began to descend, volplaning in graceful fashion. Apparently it was under the most perfect control. On reaching the earth the machine landed with no great shock, ran a short distance along the ground, and then stopped.

Rushing to the spot, the British soldiers found, to their amazement, that the pilot was dead.

So fortunate had been the aim of the Englishman that he had shot the German through the head. In his dying moments the latter had started to descend, and when he reached the earth his hands still firmly gripped the controls.

The aeroplane was absolutely undamaged, and was appropriated by the British aviators.

(3) From a *Daily Telegraph* correspondent at Rouen:

It was known that there were British wounded in Rouen—I had even spoken to one of them in the streets—but how was one to see them? The police *commissaire* sent me to his central colleague, who sent me on to the *état major*, who was anxious to send me back to him, but finally suggested that I should see the military commissary at one of the stations. He was courteous, but very firm—the authorisation I asked for could not be, and was not, granted to anyone. At the headquarters of the British General Staff the same answer in even less ambiguous terms.

It was then that Privates X., Y., Z. came to my aid. Private Z. had a request to make of me. It was that I should see to it that the black retriever of his regiment now at the front should be photographed, and that the photograph should appear in *The Daily Telegraph*.

Private Z. had a temperature of 102.5, and looked it, but he was not worrying about that. He was worrying about the photograph of the regimental retriever, which I understood him to say, though dates make it almost incredible, had gone through the Boer campaign, and had not yet had his photograph in the papers. So I met by appointment Privates X.,Y., and Z. outside the Hospice General of Rouen, and by them was franked in to the hospital, where a few dozen of our wounded were sunning themselves. It was just time, and no more, as orders had been received a few minutes before that the British wounded were to be transferred from Rouen to London, for something grave was afoot.

"Do you want to get back to England?" someone called out to a soldier whose arm was in a sling, and the whole sleeve of whose jacket had been ripped by the fragment of a shell.

"Not I," he shouted; "I want to go to the front again and get my sleeve back, and something more."

I managed to speak with two or three of the wounded as they were getting ready for the start. One of them, an artilleryman, had been injured by his horses falling on him at Ligny, I guessed it was—only guessed, for Tommy charges a French word as bravely and much less successfully than he charges the enemy. It was the same story that one hears from all, of a heroic struggle against overwhelming odds. "They were ten to one against us, in my opinion," he said. "They were all over us. Their artillery found the range by means of aeroplanes. The shell fire was terrible."

He says that it was very accurate, but that fortunately the quality of the shells is not up to that of the shooting. My informant's division held out for twenty-four hours against the overwhelming odds. Then, when the Germans had managed to get a battery into action behind, they retired during the night of Wednesday, steadily and in excellent order, keeping the German pursuit at bay. The next man I spoke to really spoke to me. He was anxious to tell his story.

"I have been in the thick of it, in the very thick of it. I was one of the chauffeurs in the service of the British General Staff."

He told me that he was not a Regular soldier, but a volunteer from the Automobile Club, an American who had become a naturalised English citizen, and had once been a journalist. His own injury, a burnt arm, was from a back-fire, but his escape from the German bullets had been almost miraculous. Three staff officers, one after another, had been hit in the body of the car behind him. This is his story:

"On Friday, the 25th, the British were just outside Le Cateau. On Saturday morning the approach of the Germans in force was signalled. On Sunday morning at daybreak a German aeroplane flew over our lines, and, although fired at by the aeroplane gun mounted in the car, and received with volleys from the troops, managed to rejoin its lines. Twenty minutes later the German artillery opened fire with accuracy. The aeroplane, as so often, had done its work as range-finder. For twelve hours the cannonade went on. Then the British forces retreated six miles. On Monday morning the bombardment began again, and at two that afternoon the German forces entered Le Cateau from which the English had retired. Many of the houses were in. flames. The Germans, who had ruthlessly bayoneted our wounded if they moved so much as a finger as they lay on the ground, were guilty of brutal conduct when they entered the city.

"On Tuesday, the British, who had retired to Landrecies, were again attacked by the Germans. They believed, wrongly, that on their right was a supporting French force. The range was again found by aeroplane, and the British were compelled to evacuate. That was on Tuesday. The British troops had been fighting steadily for four days, but their morale and their spirits had not suffered."

As I write, a detachment of the R.A.M.C. is filing past, and people have risen from their chairs and are cheering and saluting. Half an hour ago Engineers passed with their pontoons decorated with flowers and greenery. The men had flowers in their caps, and even the horses were flower-decked. Tommy Atkins has the completest faith in his leaders and in himself. He quite realises the necessity for secrecy of operations in modern warfare. Of course, he has his own theories. This is one of them textually:

"The Germans are simply walking into it. Of course, we have had losses, but that was part of the plan—the sprat to catch the whale. They are going to find themselves in a square between four allied armies, and then,"—so far Private X., but here

Private Y. broke in cheerfully; "And then they will be electro-
cuted."

And at this moment it begins to look as if—apart from that detail
of the square of four armies—Privates X. and Y. had known what they
were talking about; for some few days ago the great retreat came to an
abrupt end, the British and French forces carrying out General Joffre's
carefully laid plan of campaign, turned their defensive movement into
a combined attack, the Germans fell back before them and are still retiring. They marched through Belgium into France with heavy fighting and appalling losses, only to be held in check at the right place and
time and beaten back by the road they had come, when Paris seemed
almost at their mercy. But that retirement is another story.

6

The Spirit of Victory

He only knows that not through Him
Shall England come to shame.

Sir F. H. Doyle.

Even through those three weeks when they were retreating before the enemy, the whole spirit of the British troops was the spirit of men who are fighting to win. There is no hint of doubt or despondency in any of their letters home. They talk lightly of their hardest, most terrible experiences; they greet the unseen with a cheer; you hear of them cracking jokes, boyishly guying each other, singing songs as they march and as they lie in the trenches with shells bursting and shots screaming close over their heads. They carried out their retreats grudgingly, but without dismay, in the fixed confidence that their leaders knew what they were after, and that in due time they would find they had only been stooping to conquer. "Spratty," of the Army Service Corps, in a letter home says:

> They won't let us have a fair smack at them. I have never seen such a sight before. God knows whose turn is next, but we shall win, don't worry.

This is the watchword of them all: "*Don't worry—we shall win.*"

Private S. Browne, whilst his regiment was marching through France to the front wrote:

> Wine is offered us instead of water by the people, but officers and men are refusing it. Some of the hardest drinkers in the regiment have signed the pledge for the war.

A French soldier told a reporter at Dieppe:

Tommy goes into battle singing some song about Tip-Tip-Tip-Tipperary, and when he is hit he does not cry out. He just says 'blast,' and if the wound is a small one he asks the man next to him to tie a tourniquet round it and settles down to fighting again.

A corporal of the Black Watch explained to a hospital visitor:

It was a terrible bit of work. The Germans were as thick as Hielan' heather, and by sheer weight forced us back step by step. But until the order came not a living man flinched. In the thick of the bursting shells we were singing Harry Lauder's latest.

Trooper George Pritchard wrote to his mother from Netley Hospital the other day:

I got hit in the arm from a shell. Seven of our officers got killed last Thursday, but Captain Grenfell was saved at the same time as me. What do you think of the charge of the 9th? It is worth getting hit for.

Private J. Scott, from his place in the field writes:

We are all in good heart, and ready for the next round whenever it may come.

Corporal Brogan writes:

South Africa was child's play to what we have been through, but we are beginning to feel our feet now, and are equal to a lot more gruelling.

Private Patrick McGlade says in a letter to his mother:

We are all beat up after four days of the hardest soldiering you ever dreamt of. I am glad to say we accounted for our share of the Germans. We tried hard to get at them many a time, but they never would wait for us when they saw the bright bits of steel at the business end of our rifles. Some of them squeal like the pigs on killing day when they see the steel ready. Some of our finest lads are now sleeping their last sleep in Belgium, but, mother dear, you can take your son's word for it that for every son of Ireland who will never come back there are at least three Germans who will never be heard of again. When we got here we sang 'Paddies Evermore,' and then we were off to chapel to pray for the souls of the lads that are gone.

Corporal A. Hands writes:

> Some of us feel very strongly about being sent home for scratch-
> es that will heal. Don't believe half the stories about our hard-
> ships. I haven't seen or heard of a man who made complaint of
> anything. You can't expect a six-course dinner on active service,
> but we get plenty to fight on.

Cases of personal pluck were so common that we soon ceased to
take notice of them, a wounded driver in the Royal Artillery told an
interviewer:

> There was a man of the Buffs, who carried a wounded chum
> for over a mile under German fire, but if you suggested a Victo-
> ria Cross for that man he would punch your head, and as he is a
> regular devil when roused the men say as little as they can about
> it. He thinks he didn't do anything out of the common, and
> doesn't see why his name should be dragged into the papers
> over it. Another case I heard of was a corporal of the Fusilier
> Brigade—I don't know his regiment—who held a company
> of Germans at bay for two hours by the old trick of firing at
> them from different points, and so making them think they had
> a crowd to face. He was getting on very well until a party of
> cavalry outflanked him, as you might say, and as they were right
> on top of him there was no kidding about his 'strength,' so he
> skedaddled, and the Germans took the position he had held so
> long. He got back to his mates all right, and they were glad to
> see him, for they had given him up for dead.

A non-commissioned officer of the Buffs, writing from hospital
says:

> No regiment fought harder than we did, and no regiment has
> better officers, who went shoulder to shoulder with their men,
> but you can't expect absolute impossibilities to be accomplished,
> no matter how brave the boys are, when you are fighting a force
> from twenty to thirty times as strong. If some of you at home
> who have spoken sneeringly of British officers could have seen
> how they handled their men and shirked nothing you would
> be ashamed of yourselves. We are all determined when fit again
> to return and get our own back.

Everywhere you find that the one cry of the soldiers who are invalided home—they are impatient to be cured quickly and get back "to have another slap at them." We know how our women here at home share that eager enthusiasm in this the most righteous war Britain has ever gone into; and isn't there something that stirs you like the sound of a trumpet in such a passage as this from the letter a Scottish nun living in Belgium has written to her mother?

> I am glad England is aroused, and that the British lion is out with all his teeth showing. Here these little lions of Belgians are raging mad and doing glorious things.
> Tell father I am cheery, and feel sometimes far too warlike for a nun. That's my Scottish blood. I hope to goodness the Highlanders, if they come, will march down another street on their way to the *caserne*, or I shall shout and yell and cheer them, and forget I mustn't look out of the window.

An extract from Sergeant T. Cahill's letter to his friends at Bristol gives you a snap-shot of our women in the firing line, and of the fearless jollity and light-heartedness with which our Irish comrades meet the worst that their enemies can do:

> The Red Cross girleens, with their purty faces and their sweet ways, are as good men as most of us, and better than some of us. They are not supposed to venture into the firing line at all, but they get there all the same, and devil the one of us durst turn them away.
> Mick Clancy is that droll with his larking and bamboozling the Germans that he makes us nearly split our sides laughing at him and his ways. Yesterday he got a stick and put a cap on it so that it peeped above the trenches just like a man, and then the Germans kept shooting away at it until they must have used up tons of ammunition, and there was us all the time laughing at them.

But I think there is perhaps nothing in these letters that is more touching or more finely significant than this:
Corporal Sam Haslett writes:

> The other day I stopped to assist a young lad of the West Kents, who had been badly hit by a piece of shell. He hadn't long to live, and knew it, but he wasn't at all put out about it. I asked him if there was any message I could take to any one at home, and the poor lad's eyes filled with tears as he answered: 'I ran

away from home and 'isted a year ago. Mother and dad don't know I'm here, but you tell them that I'm not sorry I did it.' When I told our boys afterwards, they cried like babies, but, mind you, that's the spirit that's going to pull England through this war. I got his name and the address of his people from his regiment, and I am writing to tell them that they have every reason to be proud of their lad. He may have run away from home, but he didn't run away from the Germans.

And if you have caught the buoyant, heroic ardour that rings through those careless, unstudied notes our gallant fellows have written home, you know that there is not a man in the firing line who will.

With My Regiment

Contents

To "PAT"
WHO WAS KILLED IN FRONT OF LA BASSÉE ON
OCTOBER 21, 1914, THIS BOOK IS
AFFECTIONATELY DEDICATED
BY THE AUTHOR

Introduction

Report yourself to O.C. 1st Battalion at —— immediately.
—Group.

So the time had come. Of course I guessed what was going to be in the wire before I opened it, but somehow the pink telegraph envelope, and that little word Group at the end of the message, shook me out of an exciting daydream into reality. For years we had been brought up on the word "Group," which was to come at the end of the order for mobilisation. Now it was being flashed over wires all over the country. Our training was to bear fruit. The happy, careless—some people say, rather useless—life of the army officer in peacetime was over. The country had gone to war.

I was staying at the time in a large house by the banks of the Thames. My hostess was a mother of soldiers. She took the news calmly, as a mother of soldiers should; said goodbye to her eldest boy, who was to go with the first troops that left England, arranged for the outfit of her two second sons, and sent for her baby from Eton, whom she saw dispatched to the Royal Military College. It was a great house to be in on the outbreak of war—a house whose sons to the third and fourth generation had built up the British Empire, and which, now, when the Empire was called upon to fight for its life, stood firm and undismayed.

I went up to London to my rooms to collect a few things. My landlady was breathless with helping me pack, aghast at the National crisis, and rather shocked at my levity. Levity—yes, I suppose I was flippant. What else could one be when suddenly told one was going to war with Germany? I was rather enjoying the packing and everything up to a point, but as I ransacked drawers I came on a bundle of letters with some absurd comic postcards. The letters had a faint scent of violet about them. They had to be sealed up and left behind, with directions for their disposal if I didn't come back. And there was a photograph to be taken from the mantelpiece and put in a pocket-book, a photograph which had been in many places with me. Well, now it must go on its travels again. I got an aching in the back of my throat and hurried to my club for a drink.

From the club I went to the station. There was a big crowd on the platform of the boattrain. Many women had come to see their men-folk off, and some to travel with them as far as they could. There were also a great many people who were crossing over to Ireland under the impression that it would be the last night of the Channel service for civilian traffic. There were business men, and people whose homes were in Ireland, and officials. All looked a little anxious, as much as to say, "Well, it has begun!"

Our journey was uneventful until we came alongside the wharf at —— and here newsboys met us with placards:

ENGLAND DECLARES WAR ON GERMANY.

At the camp I reported myself to the adjutant. There was little in his manner to show that he was getting a regiment ready to go to war, except that he showed an indisposition to talk, and seemed trying to keep his mind clear of everything except for the sequence of things which had to be done.

After reporting to the adjutant I went across to the mess. The mess was in a state of packing. Cases, boxes, and litter of all descriptions blocked the corridors; each officer's room was like the interior of a furniture removal van, and the mess waiters were busy packing away all the regimental silver and pictures. The only things which stood out clearly from the jumble were the field-service kits of the different officers.

These were for the most part all neatly rolled up in brown or green valises ready to be thrown on the transport wagon at an instant's no-tice. Now and again an officer would come to a pair of scales outside the mess, weigh his kit, and then start frantically to undo it, pull out a pair of boots or a blanket, and roll it up again. It took some nice adjustment to get all that was wanted into the 35 lb. allowed.

The following morning we heard a band and cheering, and look-ing out of the window saw some three hundred men marching up from the station. All the regiment turned out to greet the new ar-rivals—they were fine men in the prime of life, and swung along evidently well used to pack and rifle. They were the old soldiers of the regiment—reservists who had been called back to the Colours on mobilisation from civil life.

They had been down to the depot, thrown off their civilian clothes, and taken up their rifles once more. They had most of them served under many of the officers who were still with the regiment. It put heart into all, and strengthened the general feeling of confidence that we should see the thing through, to see so many old faces coming back to march with the regiment once more.

For a night or two before the regiment embarked we dined in mess thirty strong. I used to wonder, as we sat round the table, looking at the faces of my brother officers, what fate held in store for them, how many would come back, how others would die. It was going to be "a hell of a war." All were agreed on that. There was no feeling of going off for a day's hunting about anyone. Men made their wills quietly, packed their belongings, and wrote letters of goodbye to their friends. One grey morning at six the regiment marched across the open plain behind . barracks to the little siding. A few officers' wives and those left behind came to see them off, but there was no cheering and few tears. The train stole quietly out of the station, and the regiment went to war.

"Well—see you out soon," Goyle called to me.

"Yes—I expect so," I answered, and said goodbye to him and the others.

Alas, there are few left now to read these words. The war continues. Of the survivors a half have still to serve. For me, my fighting days are done. I am not sorry. Whatever ideas I had as a cadet, this war has taught me that fighting is too fierce and heart-racking to be a sport or anything except a duty.

These sketches of war as I saw it I write once more by the banks of the upper reaches of the Thames, calm and beautiful with her fringe of browning leaves, as she was stately and magnificent in full midsummer a year before. Now autumn has come and the dead leaves lie in the golden sunlight.

Of my brother officers, who read these words, I ask only the kindly tolerance they have always shown. Should they recognize themselves in deeds described, and find fault with the accuracy of the account, will they remember that it is difficult to give chapter and verse without notes to refer to. And for notes, I think all will agree that to have taken them for such a purpose while out there would have been a waste of time.   "Platoon Commander."

1

Taking Out a Draft

I was sitting drinking a gin-and-bitters in the lounge of the big hotel facing the sea when Mulligan came dashing in. "I say, you're wanted back at the barracks at once. You've got to come out with me with the draft tonight."

"All right, old son, have a gin-and-bitters anyway. What time does the train start?"

"In an hour's time-seven o'clock," said Mulligan, still much excited, but not, however, making any attempt to move away as the waiter approached.

"Well, here's to the enterprise and our handsome selves," he said a few minutes later, raising his glass.

Mulligan was not handsome; he had a face the colour of boiled beetroot, very blue eyes, and a humorous mouth. He was a Special Reserve subaltern, who before the war had done a chequered month's training with the battalion every year, and spent the other eleven months interesting himself in aviation, theatrical life, and the motor business. To go out to the Front with him as one's colleague in charge of a draft of 180 men was a certain way of avoiding ennui.

We had been waiting some while with the reserve battalion for our turn to go out, and now, just four weeks after the regiment sailed with the vanguard of the Expeditionary Force, we were sent for at two hours' notice.

We were ready, of course. There was not much to get ready, except our 35 lb. kit, and that we always kept rolled up by our beds. Our revolvers, field-glasses, water-bottles, and haversacks were hung on our belts, and we had only to tell our servants to take our kits down to the transport wagon and walk on to the square where the draft was paraded, which we did.

The colonel said a few words, the town band fell in at the head of the column, the crowd waved goodbye, and the draft cheered and yelled and sang their way to the station. The draft was in the best of spirits; it cheered the colonel, adjutant, and any officers on sight; it leant out of the carriage windows and waved beer bottles, and rifles, and caps; and it greeted with such uproarious applause any attempt to give orders on the part of Mulligan or myself that we thought it best to remain in the corner of our first-class carriage. There were 180 men of all ages from nineteen to forty, old soldiers and young soldiers, militiamen, reservists, and a few regulars.

"We are going to have a jolly time with these," said Mulligan, indicating the draft.

Our transport was a converted Blue Line boat, which the trip before had brought over German prisoners, and the trip before that cattle from America. She had been carpentered up to carry troops, and her hold was a network of planks and scaffolding. She was to carry, besides ourselves, drafts for five other regiments, and each of these had to receive, on embarkation, rations to last for five days.

From the moment we got on board Mulligan began to prove invaluable. He collected our full number of rations from the bewildered and suspicious Army Service Corps official, he annexed an easily defended corner in the hold, stored the rations there, and put a guard over them; he frightened two other draft officers out of the only remaining officer's cabin and put our kit on to their bunks, and finally, when all was quiet, he led me to a hotel in the port where we could get a drink after ten.

The transport sailed the next morning, and once under way there was little or nothing for officers and men to do except lie about in the sun. It was a glorious September morning as we steamed past the Isle of Wight, with only two destroyers, one ahead and one to port, to remind us we were at war. But as we sat smoking and talking on deck there was a feeling in the air which dispelled the sense of being on a pleasure trip.

I think that just for those few hours as we left the shores of England there was heaviness in each man's heart. It was no holiday this we were going on. There was an officer in a Highland regiment, who was one of fifteen officers of the same regiment on their way out to replace fifteen brother officers who had only crossed the sea four weeks before: a splendid-looking fellow, with his kilt and gaily cocked Glengarry; there would be very few fellows in the regiment that he knew out there now, he said to me. He had rather a serious expression. It was grim work going out to fill the place of a friend who had been killed. And there was another fellow whom I'd known well years ago and who welcomed me with delight when he found we were to be on the same transport. "You know, I don't like this a bit," he said, evidently much relieved to find some one to whom he could speak his heart, instead of keeping up the conventional mask of joy at having been ordered to the Front. "As far as I can see, one is certain to be killed."

We talked over old days when we had been quartered near London and gone off together to Covent Garden balls and other entertainments.

"You know, I'm married now," he told me.

"You're *not?*" I said, laughing; it seems so funny when one's bachelor friends get married; and he looked just the same dog as ever.

"Yes, I've been married a year—got a brat too," he said with an air of having conclusively reformed; then, returning to the subject of the war, "absolutely certain to get hit, you know—it's all very well—never even had time to say goodbye to my wife and kid."

A month or two afterwards I saw from the papers that his regiment had been in action and lost fourteen officers—eleven wounded and three killed. It seemed just the infernal luck of the thing that he should have been one of the three killed.

The voyage lasted three days. By the middle of the second lay quite halt the troops were sea-sick. It also came on to rain. The men had therefore all to remain in the hold. Owing to the exigencies of war they had to be packed like Chinese *coolies*, and there was no room for them to walk about, barely enough for them to lie down. The boards on which they lay soon became littered with bits of biscuit, cheese, clots of jam, and fragments of bully beef. The rain found its way down to the hold through the improvised companion ways, and not more than half the men could keep dry. The stench of the hold soon became appalling. The men themselves did not seem to worry much, but lay about, those who were well enough smoking, those who were not, with the aggrieved expression Tommy often wears when he is sorely tried, as much as to say: "—— it, what next am I going to be asked to do?" But when Tommy wears this expression it by no means follows he is not going to carry out the command. He retreated from Mons in this fashion.

The sun was shining again as we arrived off the mouth of the Loire.

As we steamed slowly up the river we began to see the first signs of war. There was a large concentration camp on the left bank. We were passed and were vociferously cheered by another transport, lying off the dock with her decks thick with men waiting to be disembarked. We were eventually moored alongside a quay and told we must all remain on board till to-morrow morning. This was a disappointment to the men, a few of whom endeavoured to land on their own initiative by means of a rope ladder. A guard was put over the ladder and most of the officers retired to the saloon for drinks.

We had various distractions during the evening. First a visit from a wounded officer who had been sent down from the base camp. He said his regiment had been badly cut up. Some of the others asked him about individual officers in his regiment. "The colonel—oh, the colonel has 'gone.' Chippendale—poor Chippendale, he thought he'd been hit in the stomach and was dead. 'Curtes,' yes, Curtes I had been alongside him in the trench and I shot through the head. There was a fellow in hospital with him who had had eleven bullets in his leg. He was dying. He didn't know how long he'd be at the base camp. They had tried to put him on a hospital boat for England, but he had got off again. He thought he'd go back in a week. It was awful up there."

He was the first wounded man we had seen, and we said one to another: "By Jove, he has been through it."

Now I know that his funny way of saying everybody was dead, and the shocked look on his face, combined with the wish to go back, and "we are in for a bigger thing than we ever thought "attitude, were all symptoms of nervous strain, which most men get after a certain time in action.

Besides our visitor we saw something of the life of the town from the sides of the boat. There were a good many men in khaki coming and going along the streets and in *cafés*, apparently all rather the worse for drink, and there was an officer's picket parading the streets putting the more drunken under arrest. It was the first few days of the new base camp, and the provost-marshal was just getting the town in order.

As Mulligan and I were turning in for the night an orderly reported that a man had been drowned trying to get off the boat, and an officer was wanted to go down to the quay. Mulligan was up immediately. It seemed rather an unpleasant job for a boy like him, so I said there was no need for him to go as the man might not belong to our draft.

He grinned and put on his cap. "I think I'll go and get a sight of my first corpse," he said.

It was pouring with rain when we landed the next morning. We were told to march to No. 7*a* base camp, which we should find two miles outside the town, shown the direction, and off we started. There were the details of some five divisions quartered round the town, first reinforcements, second reinforcements, artillery units, cavalry, A.S.C., and Royal Flying Corps. As these were all divided into various small settlements, which each guarded its domain jealously and denied all knowledge of us when we offered ourselves for accommodation, it was no easy matter to arrive at the right spot. It rained steadily during our search; however, at last, after plodding through miles of tents and across a half-dried swamp, we found a small camp in la field which had a board by the guard-tent marked "7*a*."

The sergeant of the guard pointed out to me the camp adjutant's tent and, leaving the draft in charge of Mulligan, I went across to it. The men were by this time wet to the skin and, as clean sheets and pyjamas were not included in their kit, or, as a matter of fact, my change of clothing except a pair of socks and a clean shirt, it looked as though they would most of them have pneumonia the next morning. However, one thing about active service is that it eliminates most of the minor worries of life. A man who may have a bullet through him before he is many days older is not very much afraid of catching cold when he wet, and the men, when their tents were shown them, just shook the rain off their caps and turned inside.

The camp adjutant was a very fierce individual, and when I inquired about a tent for Mulligan and myself said he did not think there was one; when I asked him what then it would be best for us to do, he was first blasphemous and then completely indifferent. A tent standing by itself behind the men's lines, he said, was a cavalry officer's tent, in fact, the whole camp was really a cavalry camp, and he did not know why the —— we had been sent there.

After he had gone I decided to go and look at the cavalry officer's tent, pulling aside the flaps cautiously I peered inside and there saw, sitting on his valise and eating a biscuit with jam, a very immaculate young gentleman, with light, white-balled breeches and a large silver eagle on his cap. His head was bent as I looked in, but as he looked up I saw the pink and white, ingenious face of Herbert Beldhurst.

"Hullo!" I said.

"Hullo!" said Herbert, looking at me in polite perplexity, then, remembering who I was: "Oh, hullo! Come inside."

I entered.

"Have a cigarette?"

He produced a huge new leather campaigning cigarette case. Everything in his tent was new and designed, regardless of cost, to make campaigning as comfortable as possible. He had a smart spare saddle with two bright leather revolver holsters, a sandwich-case, a box of Fortnum and Mason's groceries, a special Burberry, and a gorgeous canary-yellow woollen waistcoat.

Hearing of our difficulty he at once offered me a share of his tent, and I had my kit put inside. Mulligan I left to look after himself, with implicit confidence in his power to do so.

Half an hour later Mulligan had billeted himself on two young officers fresh from Sandhurst, combined their rations with ours, and constituted himself president of a joint mess.

For the next few days we remained at the base camp waiting for orders to go up to the Front. The time was passed in route marching, inspecting arms and equipment, and trying to instil some sense of discipline into the draft. This last duty took some performing, as the draft resented being cooped up in the square acre of camp ground, and showed a disposition individually to go off into the town and get drunk.

One evening, about 7.30, an order came for the drafts for the 5th Division to entrain, and Mulligan and I and our 180 followers marched to the station.

That journey up to the Front was for me a never-to-be-forgotten experience. It lasted for three days, the train creeping along at ten miles an hour. As on the boat, we were a mixed party, comprising drafts for some eight regiments, and totalling about 1500 men. The train was of immense length. The senior officer was an elderly ex-Militia subaltern, completely incompetent. He made no regulations, posted no guards at stations, gave none of the draft officers orders, and by the end of the third day was firing his revolver wildly out of the window. For this I do not blame him much, for the situation had by this time reached a climax.

The different drafts remained fairly quiet in their carriages for the first night, but when the next morning broke fine and sunny and we stopped at a station in the middle of a French town, first one man and then another climbed down from the stuffy, crowded carriages on to the platform. From the platform it was only a step into the main street of the town, and this step was quickly taken. When the train wanted to move on there were no drafts. The drafts were all in *cafés*, cottages, and pie shops, receiving a hearty welcome from the inhabitants. The elderly ex-Militia subaltern said they must be collected and put back in the train, and set off with different draft officers to do this, but as fast as the men were turned out of one shop they went into another lower down the street. Eventually Mulligan organized a drive from the lower end of the town up to the station, the men were collected, and off we started again.

Warned by this experience, the ex-Militia subaltern ordered the driver of the train on no account again to stop near a town. Our next halt was, therefore, well in the middle of open country. Beside the line there ran a peaceful stream. The noonday heat was by now at its height, and after a glance out of the carriage windows we settled to sleep, secure in our remoteness from trouble. Suddenly the ex-Militia-man, putting his head out of the window, exclaimed:

"My God! Look at the ——s."

We looked, and saw several of the draft divesting themselves of their clothes preparing to bathe. We jumped out to order them into the train again, but while we were doing this every carriage was opened and the different drafts, perhaps thinking a bathing parade had been ordered and the officers were going down to superintend, all jumped out and made for the river.

"I should start the train again," said Mulligan, looking coldly on the scene of confusion. "They'll come back quick enough if they think they are going to be left behind."

The order was given, and with a long, warning whistle the train started slowly off. The effect was electrical. The men began to pour back at once. The train was kept going at two miles an hour, and those dressed were quickly on board again. One man, stark naked except for a pair of trousers, was left racing after her down the line holding up his trousers with one hand. He soon took a heavy toss over a switch wire, and the train had to be stopped and a party sent back to fetch him. While this was happening the ex-Militia subaltern in charge, who was keeping an eagle look-out all along the train, spied another man making off. He called to him to stop, but the man apparently did not hear and continued. The distracted subaltern then called on a corporal in the next carriage to fire at the culprit with his rifle, which he did.

The victim, suddenly alive to his position, gave a wild yell when the shot was fired, and ran away as hard as he could. He disappeared into a wood and was never seen again.

Nearing Paris we began to pass hospital trains going west, and outside the city were halted alongside a train-load of German prisoners. They were a miserable, abject-looking lot, huddled together on the floors of the carriages, all in their muddy grey uniforms as they had been captured. I do not think in those days there was much hate in the heart of the British Tommy towards his foe, for our fellows threw them biscuits which they devoured ravenously, and cigarettes which they lit and passed round one to another with trembling hands.

The suburban trains were running into Paris with women, and men unfit for service or over military age, much as though business was going on as usual, but we were hardly beyond the outskirts before we were passing through ground which we were told the Germans had held a few weeks before, and the impression gathered was very different from any which could be derived within fifteen miles of London.

Beyond Paris we passed through some beautiful, thickly wooded country, and were told we were within thirty kilometres of the enemy. At one point we halted by a field-ambulance station. Here the wounded were brought down from behind the firing-line in motor ambulances, their wounds dressed, and then put on to a train. It was a stern first sight of war, that long barn strewn with straw and packed with groaning, bloodstained, muddy men straight from the trenches.

2

Railhead and Beyond

For the last stage of the journey the train crawled very slowly. Very faintly in the distance we could hear the boom of guns. We looked at one another, Mulligan and I and the two lads from Sandhurst.

"We're getting into it now," said one of the Sandhurst boys.

"Yes—maybe this time twenty-four hours we shall be dead," said Mulligan with a grin.

In those days it did indeed happen that an officer only survived one day after reaching railhead. Some had been killed literally on their way to the trenches. However, Mulligan's cheery attitude of fatalism, combined with the sound of the guns, did not infect me with any wild good spirits, and I pulled out my pipe and filled it for the fifth time since lunch.

The four of us had been living for three days in the first-class carriage ever since we had entrained with our respective drafts at the base. We had slept, eaten, smoked, and made ourselves as comfortable as space would permit, and had also become very good friends. They were splendid boys, the two cadets from Sandhurst—one eighteen, the other nineteen. Theirs had been a short interval between the schoolboy and the man. A month after leaving the Royal Military College they had found themselves responsible officers sent out with a draft to their regiment in France. It had been instructive to watch the perfect self-possession of the boys and the way they handled their men.

Now as we neared our journey's end they sat calmly looking out of the window, their ears pricked to catch the sound of the distant guns, liking the thought of war perhaps no more than others do when they find themselves very near to it, but perfectly self-possessed and prepared to do whatever was required of them. They have both given their lives for their country now, poor lads—such bits of life as they had to give, having passed through only two stages of it, and never known "the lover" or the full strength of man.

At railhead the train stopped about half a mile outside the station. The railway transport officer came down the line to give us our instructions. He said he proposed to leave us in a siding for the night and we could have the train to ourselves, which would be better than turning out in a field to sleep. The men could light fires by the railway line for cooking, but they must not drink the water from a stream which ran alongside the line as it was unsafe. There were two wells from which water could be drawn for the troops a little way beyond a level-crossing further up the line. If each draft would send water-carrying parties they should be directed to the wells. He wished a guard put at the level-crossing to prevent any man walking up the line into the town.

He was with us about four minutes giving his orders concisely, and so that they could be clearly understood; then he went back towards the station to attend to the multitude of duties which fall to the lot of a railway transport officer. He spoke without flurry or excitement and gave the impression, which every staff-officer should give, of being a thoroughly capable man who knew exactly what he wanted the troops he was handling to do.

When the R.T.O. had gone we went along the line to carry out the orders we had received. Having been explicitly told that the stream was poisoned and not fit to drink, and that all fires must be lit on the right side of the line and not on the left, some of the men proceeded to light fires on the wrong side of the railway and to fill their bottles from the stream. Having put these matters right by standing about and yelling at the offenders, and things having been put more or less in shape for the night. Mulligan and I went off into the town. The town which lay deep down in a valley was in pitch darkness. There was no sign of life in the streets, except in the market square where some wagons were parked and a group of soldiers were sitting round the embers of a fire. Now and again large, silent motor-cars with officers wrapped up to the chin in overcoats and mufflers glided through.

One of the men by the wagons told us that Sir John French had been in the town half an hour ago, had a quick consultation with some general officers, and passed on. In spite of the darkness, quiet, and absence of signs of activity, one felt somehow, as one stood in that market square with the shadowy wagons and group of men round the fire, that one and crossed the border and come into the zone of war.

Railways were done with now and the infantry must take to their feet.

In view of certain reports we had heard about officers being picked off by specially detailed snipers, Mulligan and I had decided that at the first opportunity we would get rid of our brown leather belts and put on the web equipment worn by the men. Accordingly, when we got to the market square, we asked if there was any ordnance store in the town. A soldier directed us to a house at the corner of the square. We knocked on the door, and after a little difficulty roused the storeman, who took us into a large room where a quantity of clothing, equipment, and rifles collected from the dead, were piled on the floor.

The storeman was a Royal Field Artilleryman, and he told us he was one of three survivors of a battery which had been left to fight a desperate rearguard action in the retreat from Mons—it was the battery in which all but one gun were put out of action. The man had a subdued manner and was reluctant to speak much of the engagement. To us, who had not yet seen a shell burst, this meeting with a man who had been through so much fighting was significant. We took our web equipment and made our way back to the train.

The morning broke fine and sunny, and we turned out along the line quite ready to march. As we were putting on the web equipment we had collected over night, the French driver of the train came along. He stopped and looked at us curiously, then asked why we were discarding our officer's belts and putting on men's equipment. We explained it was because we did not want to be picked out as officers. He said: "With our officers it is the same uniform in peace as in war." I could not think of an adequate reply to this, but the natural and irritable one would have been "more fools they," which Mulligan made without any hesitation. However, the engine driver's remark rankled, and as the R.T.O. said that most of the officers he had seen had gone up to the front in their Sam Browne belts, we decided to do the same after all and pack the web equipment in our kit.

We got our orders to march at noon. Mulligan and I with our draft and the draft for another regiment were to start first; the two Sandhurst lads, who were going to another brigade, were to wait till the afternoon. We sorted out our different drafts, wished them goodbye, and set off.

Part of the way from railhead to divisional headquarters lay over a ridge which overlooked the valley of the Aisne. From this ridge we saw our first shells bursting at a comfortable distance of some two mile away. One wondered as one watched the little white puffs of smoke which appeared suddenly and noiselessly, hovered for a minute a score of feet above the earth, and blew away, what damage they had caused and what it must be like for the men who formed the target beneath them.

The valley of the Aisne, as we saw it, except for those white puffs of smoke and the occasional distant boom of a heavy gun, showed no signs of war. The fields were quiet and empty as on a Sunday, with crops growing tranquilly and here and there a stack of hay. At one point we passed an artillery supply park with an imperturbable-looking gunner subaltern, with an eyeglass, and a major in charge. The major had a large scale-map of the area, and showed me from it where our lines and the German's lines lay, pointing out the actual places on the horizon.

He was passing the time making out possible phases of battles to come from the map. The subaltern told us that the word "Uhlan" (in the early days of the war often heard) was extinct as a form of terrorism, for, he said, they and their horses were half-starved, and turned and bolted on sight.

After some five miles march we arrived at divisional headquarters, which consisted of the principal house in a tiny village. Here I found an officer in my regiment who was attached to the staff, and who asked me to come in and have tea while he found out what I was to do with the men I had brought out from England.

The general and his staff were having tea round a deal table in the front room of the house when I went in and all greeted me kindly. Tea consisted of bread, jam, and tea without milk. There was no butter, only two or three plates, and some brown sugar in a paper bag. The meal belied any impression I may have had of the luxury in which generals and their staff were wont to live in wartime.

There was a discussion among the staff officers as to what they were to do with the draft and myself and Mulligan. One was for sending us down to the trenches that night, another for keeping us back in reserve. I personally hoped for a night in peace and quiet, and I could see that the staff officer who was in favour of keeping us in reserve thought it would be rather a severe experience for a draft to be sent down into the trenches the first night they arrived at the front.

Eventually it was decided that we should go to our second line transport which lay some two miles behind the firing-line, and with directions as to the road we started off. It was by this time dark; however, we had no difficulties until we came to the village where our second line transport was supposed to be. This village was packed with troops, and from no one could we get information about the whereabouts of our second line transport. There followed an hour of hopeless wandering and questioning, while Mulligan and I cursed the army and everything to do with the army (with especial reference to the staff) for fools and worse.

At one point we came into collision with a regiment marching out to take its turn in the trenches. The officers all were wearing Burberrys and mufflers, and had greatcoats rolled on their backs. The men were carrying little pots for cooking, extra *bandoliers* of ammunition, and other things likely to be useful to them in the trenches. All looked prepared to be thoroughly uncomfortable.

At last, after some further wandering, we struck boldly out on a road along which we were told we should find our second line transport. I was a little uneasy as we left the village behind us and marched out into the darkness, for I knew we were going in the direction of the enemy, and it would be a never-to-be-forgotten episode in an officer's career to lead a draft of reinforcements fresh from England straight into the hands of the enemy instead of to their regiment. However, before we had gone far a voice greeted me cheerily and I discovered our quartermaster.

"You come with me, I'll take you to the transport. Now then, lads, close up there," he said, in the crisp, businesslike voice I had often heard on the parade-ground in times of peace when he was regimental sergeant-major.

Only those young officers who served in the days before the war, and learnt to lean a little on the "backbone" of the army, can understand the relief it was to me, after a fortnight's responsibility with the 180 rascals who formed my draft, to feel them gripped once again by the voice of an old regular ex-non-commissioned officer.

Under Clay's guidance the draft followed like sheep into the courtyard of a farm, and stood quietly in their ranks while we went into the building. In the centre of the yard a fire was burning and the sergeant-cook was busy preparing supper (this would have been too much for the draft altogether if they had been alone with me). The sergeant-cook shook my hand warmly in his huge red paw and wished me luck on joining the regiment on active service. He then busied himself preparing a dixie of tea for the men.

Inside the farm I found Sergeant Mace, the officers' mess sergeant, in khaki and shirt sleeves but just as anxious that the officers should have everything they wanted as he had been when his portly chest had been covered by a glossy white shirt. He brought me a cup of tea, unearthed from the mess van a bottle of rum, poured it liberally into the tea, and went out with some bread, dripping, and eggs to fry some supper over the fire in the yard.

Of the welcomes I have had I shall always remember the first night when I reached the second line transport of my regiment in France.

Thinking to remain with the transport that night. Mulligan and I had found some straw for the draft and were sitting on biscuit boxes over the fire drinking hot rum and water, and hearing the gossip of the regiment from Clay and Mace before turning in, when an orderly arrived with orders. We were to go down into the trenches that night.

Clay said it was rough luck we should not get one night's rest. He was also extremely matter of fact . He roused the men from their slumber in a trice, cursed a man roundly who dropped his rifle, harangued the draft in a hoarse whisper, telling them that they were going to be sent across to the other side of the river into the firing-line, and that if they made a noise they would get a German battery turned on them, said a few words to Mulligan and myself aside, advising one of us to keep at the head of the company and one behind, and to keep the men well closed up, as if fire was suddenly opened at night on troops just out of England it might be touch and go what would happen, and said goodbye to us, without—as I thought, considering the occasion—much tenderness.

It was pitch dark when we started off from the transport to go down to the firing-line. The transport sergeant came with us to show the way and marched with me at the head of the draft. He told me that he had to take the supply-wagon down every night to the regiment, and that it was a job he was glad to have over for the day. That morning he had been late returning, and day was breaking as he crossed the river. Three shells had been fired, two narrowly missing his wagon. I could see he was rather shaken by his morning's experience and that he did not particularly relish the task of piloting down the draft. However, never having seen any shells burst, they had no terror for me, and I rather enjoyed the quiet sense of adventure which hung over the expedition.

After half a mile we left the main road and crossed the pontoon bridge. From this point onwards our way lay across the fields. In the darkness we could see nothing and had no compass to give the direction. The transport sergeant picked his way by keeping to a muddy track which had been worn across the fields and stubble by troops passing to and fro from the firing-line to the rear. Whenever our boots stopped squelching and slipping back we knew we were off the track and groped about till we were back in the mud and cart-ruts again.

A few months afterwards when I read that the French troops, who had taken over our line when the British Army was moved up to Flanders, had had to retire to the high ground south of the Aisne owing to the impossibility of keeping up communication with their line across the river when the winter rain came, I remembered that muddy, slippery walk and understood their difficulties.

We had been going for what seemed quite an hour when we came to a large hay shed. Here we halted as the sergeant said he was not quite sure where we were wanted, but that the trenches were quite near. It was late, the men tired, and the hay-shed presented at any rate a certainty of shelter and some warmth, so I decided to remain there for the night.

3

Early Days on the Aisne

There was a big difference between the first and second occasions on which I joined my regiment. The first time was as a Sandhurst cadet and I joined a regiment at full strength of officers and men. I remember we sat down to dinner that night some twenty of us, and being bewildered by all the faces and trying to make out which was the colonel and wondering if I should ever learn the names of all the different subalterns and captains. The mess table was laden with silver and outside a band in scarlet tunics played.

The second time was when I rejoined after a year s absence on the outbreak of war, and went with Mulligan and the draft to join them in the trenches on the Aisne. By then they had fought at Mons, Le Cateau, and the Marne.

The adjutant, who met me behind the lines to take me to the commanding officer prepared me a little for what to expect.

"Blain is commanding," he said, as we threaded our way single file down a path through a wood. Blain, I knew, had been a very junior captain a month before when war broke out.

The adjutant proceeded to explain: "The colonel and Ames were hit at Mons." (Ames was the senior major.) Johnson and Hewett (another major and a captain) had been hit on the Marne. "Clark and Sergeant Johnson—you remember Johnson?" I nodded, well remembering Clark's inimitable colour-sergeant—the pair had been inseparable and the officer greatly dependent on the man for the keeping of his company accounts, etc., in the days of peace—"were killed the day before yesterday. They are buried together by that farm." The adjutant softened his voice from the tone of matter-of-fact recital as he pointed to a farm building through the trees.

"Well, here we are," he said as we came to a little straw and earth

138

shelter in the wood. "Here's some fresh blood, sir," he said, to a youthful looking captain sitting on a tree stump outside the shelter. This was Blain, who through the accidents of war was now left in command of the regiment. There were left, besides, one other captain and some half-dozen subalterns. Of these the scout officer and machine-gun officer were with Blain, the others out in command of their companies in the trenches.

"Hullo!" said Blain, holding out his hand. "We are going to put you with Goyle's company."

I grinned as unconcernedly as I could. So Goyle was one of the survivors, then. Goyle was the regimental fire-eater. He had been longing for this war for years and was more pleased than many others I knew when it actually happened. To be Goyle's subaltern on active service, I had always surmised, was to have guarantee of plenty of fighting.

If ever a reluctant youth found himself holding out against overwhelming odds in an impossible position it would be one of Goyle's subalterns.

"Goyle has had bad luck with his subalterns," said Blain. "He has lost four."

"I hope he doesn't lose me," I said with some sincerity.

Blain and the adjutant laughed. "Well, we'll send you on up to him," said the former. "Let's see—I think he has got the forward trench today."

"Yes, he has," said the adjutant; then, turning to me, "You'll be near enough to them for your first day in the trenches—two hundred yards."

I grinned again as genially as possible.

"Have some breakfast before you go up," said the C.O., handing me a biscuit and a pot of jam and pointing to a pannikin of tea.

It was very damp in the wood. The trees were dripping. The tea was cold. The party, with Blain as C.O., and the adjutant and two subalterns, were a forlorn little group to be left out of a regiment. All had rather a strained air, and my good spirits and feeling of being fresh out from England were evidently not infectious to men who had been through what they had. They had had a shell near them already that morning and were all frankly apprehensive of another. From that moment any ideas I may have had about the pleasures and excitements of active service left me, and I merely wondered what sort of a trench I was going to and what Fate might have to bring me on my first day of active service.

139

I had always imagined that trenches were only approached by night, and then by crawling on one's belly along narrow communication passages. But we set off in broad daylight, at eight in the morning, to go up to our trench. The reason we were able to do this was because the trenches on the Aisne were along the edges of woods, and it was possible to move through the trees right up to within two hundred yards of the enemy without being observed.

The advanced trench which Goyle was holding with his company lay in a small wood, rather in advance of the main line of trenches. The path which led to it twisted and twined and branched off into other paths so confusedly that I wondered how the adjutant could find his way. The actual trench itself consisted in a bank along the edge of the wood in which a chain of dugouts had been excavated. We found Goyle in a dugout in the centre, which was distinguished from the others by some straw and a couple of waterproof sheets; there was also a wooden box without a lid, in which the officers' rations were kept. Goyle was sitting in the dugout with Evans, his remaining subaltern, and having taken me thus far, the adjutant returned to the C.O.

Evans was an old friend of mine and fellow-subaltern. We talked together for a while and then he showed me cautiously how to creep up to the top of the parapet and look through some long grass at the enemy's trenches 200 yards away, and he told me the story of the fight for the position we now held and where so-and-so, and so-and-so—brother officers whom I'd seen leave England a month before with a cheery wave of the hand for me and a joke about meeting "out there" soon—had been killed the day before.

At nine o'clock we rummaged in our ration-box and made breakfast off jam and biscuits and cheese. It was quite pleasant in the dugout and there was no sound of war. As we were making our breakfast a shot rang out and there was a piercing yell.

"Hullo! they must have got one of the fellows I put on sentry at the edge of the wood," said Goyle, helping himself to more jam.

"Is that one of our fellows?" he called to the sergeant.

"Yessir—hit in the buttocks, sir;" the sergeant slapped the portly part of himself on which he sat.

We all laughed.

The yell gave way to groans—loud, long, and terrible.

I looked as unconcerned as possible and dipped my own biscuit into the pot. "Tell that fellow to stop making such a noise," said Captain Jones, angrily putting his head round the dugout.

I felt myself that it was a pity the Germans should know the good result of their shooting and that the fellow ought not to make such a fuss. However, the groaning went on as loudly as ever, and at last Jones got up exasperated to go and see what was the matter.

He came back with a grave face.

"Only hit in his 'sit-upon,' wasn't he?" My fellow-subaltern looked up smiling.

"H'm, it's worse—went through and has lodged somewhere in his intestines," and murmuring "in agony, poor fellow!" Captain Jones looked to see if we had emptied the jam-pot while he was away.

It did not take more than an hour or two I to pick up the rudiments of trench life. We passed the morning sitting in the dugout, reading a few old papers and smoking and I talking. By eleven the sun was high enough to peep in over the top of the parapet and warm us, and it all seemed to me a very pleasant, lazy sort of existence. There was no firing except for an occasional "*ping*" from a sniper Goyle kept posted at the corner of the trench, and an answering shot or two from the German side. Rifle fire seemed a matter of tacit arrangement. When our sniper was joined by a friend, or fired two or three times in a minute instead of once every three or four, the German fire grew brisker and life in the trench less tranquil. Our sniper was thereupon reproved by Goyle and was silent, whereupon the German fire died down.

At midday Goyle suggested we should lunch, and Evans pulled the wooden box towards him. He gave us out each two large square army biscuits and opened a small tin of bully beef, which he turned out on a piece of paper and cut into three portions. The beef and biscuits did not make a bad meal at all, but the best was to follow. Goyle produced from his haversack a tin cup, and from the box a wine-bottle about a third full. He then mixed a tot of rum with the same quantity of water in the cup and drank, passing on the emptied cup to Evans, who took his share; after I had had mine there was just enough left for us each to have half a cup more. How delicious that rum was! I rolled myself a cigarette, lay back in the straw, and basked contentedly. I felt comfortable and warn and drowsy.

Away in the distance one could hear the booming of big guns which went on all day, but this was the only thing to remind one that one was in the middle of the battle of the Aisne. I saw Evans opposite me lean back and close his eyes, and remember thinking Goyle was rather energetic to sit so bolt upright all the time.

It was a sound of firing that woke me. *Phizz—Phizz—Phizz!* through the leaves above and some sharp crack from our men. Goyle and Evans were still sitting where they had lunched, listening intently. I sat up, too, wondering what was going on. "Were we being attacked or what was happening?" I asked Goyle, who replied briefly that he did not know.

"Just take No. 8 platoon and line that trench along the end there," he said to Evans. Evans got up and crept out of the dugout along towards the sound of firing.

"Very exposed here," muttered Goyle to himself. "C.O. said if this point went the whole line would go too."

"Um!" I thought to myself, now quite alive to being in the middle of a battle.

"Are you all right?" a voice called. We looked out and saw the C.O. standing in the wood behind us. He had come running up as soon as he heard the firing. I have always remembered him running up like that to see if all was well. Many commanding officers would have thought it best to remain at their headquarters and let reports come in to them from the different companies.

It gave one great confidence to see him standing there calmly. Then suddenly the firing died down.

"Don't think it was anything," said Goyle, "but it is rather a nasty place this; we could not do much if they tried to rush us. I'll keep that platoon out along the flank there for a bit."

"You're going to be relieved tonight," said the C.O. "The Gloucesters are taking over from us."

At ten o'clock that night the company of the regiment which was relieving us filed slowly into our trenches. As each of the new platoons got into position the old platoon made its way out to the place where it had been directed to halt. There could be no talking or asking of questions as the enemy were two hundred yards away, but the simple and explicit instructions which Goyle had given to the platoon commanders in the afternoon enabled the whole movement to be carried out correctly. The section-commander of the leading section of each platoon had to keep in touch with the section commander of the rear section of the platoon in front of him, and by this plan of following my leader the whole company moved as one man in the darkness along the intricate paths which intersected the wood.

By eleven o'clock we had arrived safely at our destination—a clearing in the wood about half a mile behind the front trenches.

There we found a series of little straw houses made by the last regiment, wide enough to hold six men laying down and high enough to allow a man to sit up in them. We selected one of these bivouacs for ourselves and distributed the men among the remainder. I so far had escaped having to spend a night in the trenches, but to the men, who had been where I joined them that morning for three days and nights, the bivouacs were a great comfort. The mere relief of tension, which the extra six hundred yards or so we had put between ourselves and the enemy afforded, was appreciated by all, and being now well screened from view we could move about as we liked.

Evans told me that Goyle had hardly slept at all any of the three nights, but spent the whole time going round seeing that the sentries were alert and at their posts. After we had chosen our bivouac and put down our haversack and water-bottles to mark the place where we proposed to sleep, the question arose of supper. We had very little of our day's rations left—however, I saw a dim light peeping from a bivouac which stood by itself, and guessing it meant a party, went across to investigate. Here I found the other officers of the regiment lying round on straw discussing a cold leg of mutton and some bread which had been sent down from the transport. I claimed and was given a share for Goyle, Evans, and myself, and also a small extra tot of rum. Nothing tastes nicer than cold meat and bread when one is hungry, and with the rum and mutton inside us and a few whiffs of a pipe we were soon fast asleep.

We slept till well after six the next morning, and when we woke the sun was breaking through the mist which always haunts the valley of the Aisne at dawn. By nine a glorious autumn day had fully broken. We had two canteens of steaming tea and cold bacon for breakfast. Goyle then produced some cleaning traps and began a prodigious toilet. He shaved himself, he washed his teeth, he soaped his head and plunged it into a bucket of cold water; finally he took off his trousers and poured the water over himself. Then he had a rub down with a tiny towel, put on his trousers and shirt again, and sat down under s tree, saying he felt better. Evans and I, unshaven, muddy, but feeling quite warm and comfortable, watched all this rather cynically.

"Always wash when you get the chance," said Goyle, who, having been through the South African War, played the *rôle* of old campaigner.

It seemed to me that it would be time enough to wash the next day when we were to go back to billets. However, after half an hour

Evans sent for a bucket of water, washed himself, and declared he felt much fresher. He then joined Goyle under the tree and combed his hair. I began to feel a dirty fellow, and finally borrowing Goyle's soap and towel, washed too.

We passed the day very happily sitting about and sleeping in the sun. At dusk we got orders to move and go and improve some entrenchments.

As soon as it was dark the regiment paraded and moved off, with orders to dig till midnight and then rest and cross the Aisne an hour before dawn.

The place assigned to my company for digging was a ditch running along a fence facing the hills on the enemy's side of the river. The enemy had their trenches on the slopes of these hills, and it seemed funny to be digging under their noses, as it were, under cover of darkness. Evidently the night was good enough cover, for not a shot was fired to disturb us at our work. I noticed, however, that Goyle ran no risk, but made each man lay his equipment and rifle exactly in front of him so that the different working parties could be transformed into a firing-line at an instant's notice. The men worked away with a will as unconcerned as if they were digging a potato patch. The only thing which worried them a little was a searchlight which the enemy continually flashed across ;he front of their lines.

At first the men could not get used to this light, but threw themselves flat on the ground whenever it appeared in their direction, but as the enemy never fired, apparently the searchlight revealed nothing to them. Evans and I studied this light for a little while and then discovered that a knoll lay between it and us, and hid us from its direct rays so that we were all perfectly safe. As a matter of fact Goyle explained that if a man did come into the direct ray of a searchlight, he would only look like the stump of a tree or a shrub to the observer if he stood still. It was by movement alone that he betrayed himself. However, it requires a certain amount of confidence to stand quite still when caught by a searchlight and not try to move away or hide behind a tree.

This confidence the men who were not hidden by the knoll lacked at first; in fact, they had a great dislike for the searchlight and were inclined to be reproachful because we had no searchlights ourselves. Thomas Atkins is a keen critic of the art of war, and such things as well-placed searchlights and the superior number of the enemy's machine-guns do not escape his notice. He likes to feel that he has been given as good a start as the man he is fighting against, and it would have been interesting to have heard the comments of our men in the trenches when the Germans first started to employ gas.

At midnight we knocked off digging and retired to a field to sleep. It is extremely cold in the Aisne valley on autumn nights, and the dew-drenched ground did not look inviting. The men were told to lie down where they were, and as it began to dawn on them that no further arrangements were to be made for their comfort, they grinned rather expressively in a way they have when they wish to be quite pleasant but at the same time feel they have a lot to put up with.

I happened to have noticed the field as we passed it on our way to entrench, and to remember that at the top there were several sheaves of corn.. Accordingly, when all was quiet, I sent the men of my platoon up two at a time to fetch some of these sheaves down and also to bring me three for myself. Spreading out one underneath me and the other two over my feet and chest I soon was as warm as if I'd been between blankets.

It was a glorious night, and it was grand to be there in the warm straw looking up at the stars. About four I was awoken by a sound of stamping, and looking sideways saw the men who had no straw stamping to keep themselves warm and looking reproachfully at my platoon who were all lying snug and comfortable like a litter of puppies. Soon after this the order came to move and we crossed back over the Aisne as day was breaking. The slow-running, mist-hung river was a peaceful-looking object to give a name to a battlefield, but the putting up of the pontoon bridge by which we crossed had cost many men their lives and brought to one the V.C.

4

In Billets

The village where we were to billet lay a mile on the other side of the river in a deep quiet valley. The quartermaster and transport officer met us half a mile from our destination. They were both unaffectedly glad to see the regiment coming back into safety for a while, though, alas, there were only two-thirds of the officers left who had crossed the river a week before. It was a trying time for the quartermaster and transport subaltern, when the regiment went into action. They had to stay behind, with only occasional fleeting visits to the firing-line, often for as long as a week or ten days. When there was a big attack, and the air for miles on either side was filled with one reverberating crash of gun and rifle fire, they had to bear the strain which is always more acute for those within sound but not in sight of fighting.

"I've got a fine breakfast for you," said the quartermaster, "bacon and eggs and sausages."

We were glad to hear it. Meals for the past week had been scrappy affairs. Since we had parted company with our transport we had none of us tasted a hot dish of any description. Cold bacon and bread for breakfast, cold bully and cheese for lunch, cold bully and cheese again for supper. Good enough nourishment, Of course, for anyone, and nice enough at the time to eat, but still a real steaming dish of bacon and eggs did sound delicious.

We soon came to the village where the brigade was to be billeted in reserve. It lay in a curve of a winding valley which ran down into the main valley of the river. The billets were allotted by companies, so much cottage and farm space being given to each company commander for his company. To those who read these lines in England the quarters allotted to men back for a few days rest from trenches may not sound very grand. My company had, for instance, a stable, two

146

farm outbuildings, and a sort of underground cellar which was approached by a narrow arch—to crawl through which the men had to go on hands and knees—and which looked just like the kennels of a pack of foxhounds. The stable, the cellar, and the outhouses were bare except for a layer of straw. However, to the men these places seemed amply satisfying. They meant warmth at night, shelter from rain, and soft dry lying.

It was the first rest the men had had for some while. Many of them had lost their greatcoats, cardigans, and woollen underclothing, owing to the exigencies of actual fighting, and had had nothing to add to their scanty clothing as they lay out in the open during the cold nights. They crowded joyfully into their billets as Goyle and I and Evans went round allotting so much space to each platoon.

Having arranged for the men we now looked round for quarters for ourselves. Goyle, whose natural inclinations for Spartan simplicity were being rapidly fanned to a mania by active service, suggested that he and Evans and I should share the stone-slabbed floor of the lower room of a cottage which looked out on a manure yard. Evans, always anxious to please, was quite agreeable to this, and set to work with a broom to sweep out the yard, but I broke away from the arrangements and went to look for quarters for myself. After a short search I came on Mulligan, who had found some quite good quarters in a cottage. He had got a small bedroom leading off the owner's room, and suggested that the apple-loft on the same floor would do for me if I had one of the mattresses from his bed. I therefore sent Jenkins for my kit and set up house with him.

The 35-lb. kit which officers are allowed to keep with the transport meets all requirements on active service. As first bought and taken out from England it is a most immaculate and neatly arranged affair, but after a fortnight's jolting around in the wagons and a few hurried packings and unpackings it becomes a mere bundle containing a few cherished necessities. My valise held a sleeping-bag, two shirts, two pairs of socks, a pair of boots, a pair of trousers, some slippers, a few sticks of chocolate and a tin of tobacco. However, as Jenkins unpacked I watched it with the complacency of a man regarding his home.

A bucket of cold water and a canteen of hot were next produced, and from the sleeping-bag my toilet set—razor, shaving brush, cake of soap, comb, and toothbrush—wrapped in a towel; and removing my coat and boots and *puttees* I sat down on the valise and shaved. A bath followed in the bucket and then getting into clean socks and shirt and putting on the clippers and trousers for greater comfort, I combed my hair and surveyed myself with satisfaction in a small pocket mirror. Burnt by the sun and hardened by outdoor life, I certainly have never felt fitter in all my life.

It was now about noon, and Mulligan and I strolled across to the mess. The mess consisted chiefly of "Black Maria," a small lumbering van which the mess sergeant had bought for two pounds in Belgium at the beginning of the war, and which carried all our provisions. We were only able to gather round "Black Maria" at such times of comparative peace as being in billets or on the march behind the firing-line, but her presence on the scene always meant a scale of meals and comfort undreamed of in the trenches. Bacon and eggs came from her inside, and joints and vegetables, cocoa, tea, jam, bread, butter, biscuits, also vermouth, whisky and other stimulating drinks. It was wonderful the amount she held. We found "Black Maria" had been drawn up in the yard of a farm. A long trestle-table was set outside the front door of the farm, and several officers were sitting round this untying parcels and reading letters which had been sent out in a mail from England.

Over a fire on the far side of "Black Maria" the mess sergeant and his assistants were cooking lunch.

With the parcels which had just arrived from England there was now a plentiful supply of cigarettes, tobacco, socks, and underclothing for everybody, and while we sat waiting for lunch various exchanges were made between officers: a pair of socks for twenty-five cigarettes, an electric torch for a new briar pipe, and so on. Others, who had more of the same things sent than they wanted, put them into a box reserved for general use, from which any officer could take anything that he wanted. The parcels of officers who had been wounded and gone home were opened unceremoniously and their contents divided among the survivors. With letters from wives and sweethearts and friends in their pockets, plenty of newspapers and parcels, and the thought of having nothing to do for the next day or two, everybody was in the best of tempers at luncheon.

True, there were gaps now round the table, gaps which had not been there a few days ago, and which each was causing its measure of desolation to some English home, but by the men who had come through and learnt to bow their heads to the laws of chance and feel thankful that they too had not been taken, these gaps were not felt keenly—it was all a part of war, just as being in billets was. A day or two ago the men round the table had beer in the woods across the river fighting: then the gaps had been made: that had been no joke—now they were sitting comfortably in the sun with food before them such as they had not seen for a fortnight. It would be silly not to eat and be merry.

My apple-loft proved a most comfortable chamber, and I lost no time after dinner in throwing off my clothes, getting into pyjamas, and rolling myself up in my sleeping-bag. In the middle of the night as it seemed, or to be precise, at 4 a.m.—I was woken by Jenkins. He bore the unwelcome news that the regiment was to be on the march in a quarter of an hour. He added that he had heard a report that the Germans had broken through our line somewhere, and that the whole brigade was turning out. It was an affair of three minutes to get into my clothes and equipment, which I kept ready laid out beside me. While I was dressing, Jenkins deftly rolled and strapped my valise, and off he went with it to the transport wagon while I hurried to my company.

The company had already turned out when I arrived, and the men were standing outside their billets. Five minutes later we had formed fours and were swinging out of the village. It was quick work at night to turn a whole brigade out of billets at twenty minutes notice, for to wake 4000 sleeping men, scattered all over a village, and get each in his proper place complete with arms and equipment in that space of time, is no easy task. In peace time the operation would have taken at least three hours, for the men would not have exactly lent themselves to the project, but in war all is vastly different. The alarm proved false, and after marching for a mile we were halted and finally marched home again, this time for five days of unbroken rest.

The days passed pleasantly enough. There were so many little luxuries which could be indulged in in billets. It was good to go about feeling washed, and delightful to wake up in the morning feeling one had had a good night's rest, drink a cup of tea in bed, and then roll a cigarette and smoke it as one shaved squatting on one's mattress. Breakfast would follow at the table outside the farm—breakfast of eggs and bacon and as much tea and bread and butter and jam as one wanted. Then a visit to the company and an inspection of the men's rifles or their kit, perhaps a journey to the quartermaster to try and get a man another pair of boots or a coat which he wanted.

The men nearly all needed one thing or another renewed, and from where we were we could get fresh supplies up from the base. It was a pleasure to see the joy a man took in a new cardigan waistcoat or a clean pair of socks and a shirt. He had probably worn his old ragged things uncomplainingly for three weeks, but now he strutted about round the billets patting his chest and showing off the new waistcoat or boots to his pals.

At midday a mail often came in with packets of letters and parcels for everybody, and the letters had to be answered and the parcels opened and their contents shown round.

Then we did a little entertaining with the other regiments of the brigade, and staff officers would come down with bits of gossip and information about the general situation which we never got a chance of learning in the trenches. There was one fellow, an intelligence officer—heaven knows what has become of him now—who came to dine with us one night before going on to the trenches. His was most difficult and dangerous work, as he used to go out at nights, crawl out beyond our trenches and find out the position of the enemy's wire entanglements and advanced posts. It was the joke to tell him that a place would be laid for him at breakfast on his way back to general headquarters the next morning, and glad we all were when he came back to fill it.

Sometimes after tea we would go for short excursions to the country round. It was very beautiful country, and from the high ground on either side of the valley it was possible to get a far-reaching view of the battlefield.

Some evenings there seemed no sign of war, and one evening in particular I remember when I had gone out with Mulligan to explore a village on the hill above us. The village was built of grey stone hewn from a quarry in the hillside. Most of the inhabitants had stayed in their homes although the German had at one time been through their village. They told us how the Uhlans had ridden through in a great hurry, snatching what they wanted, but happily unable to stay to carry out coarse threats, and how the British cavalry had followed hot on their heels. But all this had been some while ago, and for the past week the village had been in peace. The church had some beautiful stained-glass windows which were all shivered by the explosion of shells, but the building itself stood intact, and Mulligan and I went inside and stepped softly up the aisle, unswept since war began, and littered with fragments of plaster from the ceiling.

There was a great sense of calm and dignity about the little church, which had remained so near the battlefield a quiet place of refuge for its people. The old priest came across from his cottage and, bowing to us ceremoniously, offered us each a pear. We walked with him through the village till we came to a point beyond, from which we could see right down into the valley where the two armies lay facing each other. The sun was just setting at the further end of the valley and the evening mists were curling low over the meadows and river. Some-where away behind a bell tolled for a service. For a few minutes as we stood there all was peace and quiet, then from the hill opposite our guns opened fire. The shell went screaming across the valley tearing their way through the soft evening air. We watched, wondering what was their target. Then suddenly flames broke out from a village lying across the valley within the enemy's lines. Looking through our glasses we could see the flames came from some stacks near a farm.

Crash—Crash—Crash! Shell after shell fell among the cottages. Slowly the flames spread as one building after another was set aflame. The sun had sunk now and the sky was darkening. The whole vil-lage seemed one crackling bonfire. Still our guns hurled shells into the flames. Their fire seemed merciless as they lashed the little village with round after round. Suddenly the firing stopped. It had grown dark. The village was blazing now fiercely, and the whole sky was red. The work of the guns was done. We stood a moment watching the lurid, glowing mass. Mulligan wondered if we had caught a nest full of German troops. The old priest said nothing: it was war. Gradually the flames grew less, and only here and there bright red patches reflected themselves against heavy clouds of smoke. Saying goodnight to the priest we made our way slowly back to billets.

5

The Move Up (1)

We had been in our billets in the village behind the Aisne a week when the order came to move. It came suddenly one evening at seven o'clock, as orders do at the Front, and by seven-thirty we were on the march. Where to, why, or for how long no one had any idea. Perhaps we were moving to a threatened point of the line, perhaps troops were being concentrated for an attack, perhaps the whole division, which had suffered heavily since the outbreak of war, was being replaced by a fresh division and was being sent back to the base to refit, reorganise, and fill its gaps.

As we marched along we attempted to make deductions from the direction we were taking. One thing was plain, the road led directly back from the line of the river and the enemy. It might be, of course, that after going a mile or two we should swing right-handed and move along parallel to the enemy but out of reach of their guns till we came behind some point where we were wanted, and then be moved up again. We climbed up out of the valley and crossed a high plateau of waste land. Goyle told me that the German rearguard of horse artillery and cavalry had dashed pell-mell across this plateau in their retreat from the Marne, hotly pursued by our cavalry and guns, pausing at intervals to exchange shots with their pursuers, crashing on down the valley and across the Aisne, where they had made the stand they had maintained ever since. It must have been a fine sight to have seen the pursuer and pursued crossing the plateau.

Four or five miles back we passed some troops bivouacking by a farm.

"What are you?" called Goyle.

"The ——s," came a rather sullen answer.

It was the —— Regiment—all that was left of it—perhaps a hundred men. They had been badly cut up a few days before, and, no longer existing as a regiment, had been withdrawn from the firing-line.

A mile or two further on we came to the end of our journey for that day—a village where we were to billet. Our billeting officer had gone ahead, and we had not long to wait in the road before he came to show the company their billeting area. In the darkness it took a little time to get the men settled. They naturally resented being put in pigsties, which Edwards, who had no sense of smell and only felt the straw with his feet, tried to do with his platoon. Then Mulligan, who was always a bit hot on these occasions, annexed a barn, which was just within our boundary, for A Company, and, successful in this, attempted to take over a kitchen right in the heart of our area for the use of A Company officers.

When I went to eject him from this he adopted the tone, "We must all share in on service," and as I still preserved a stony counte-nance, obtruded the nose of a bottle of rum from his haversack and said we would have some hot toddy when all was quiet, whereupon, on striking a bargain that I should have the bed and he a mattress from it on the floor, I let him remain.

Some electric torches we had had sent out from England were of the greatest use at times like this, as they enabled us to flash them into the interior of barns and get the men properly settled in places where there was room for them and where they could sleep in comfort. Also, as we were well away from the firing-line, we could have "Black Maria," our mess van, with us, and hot meals when we got in and be-fore we started in the morning.

We remained in the village all the next day, moving off just before nightfall the following evening. During the day I went to pay a visit to some of the other units of the brigade. The Westshires were billeted further down the village, and had passed the night as comfortably as ourselves, but the Dorchesters had not been so fortunate, and had had to sleep in a field, as there had been no billeting space left for them. Greatly conscious of the warm bed I had just left, I surveyed with a sympathy which they did not seem to appreciate the little "boovey-hutches" and lairs of straw which they had made for themselves. The artillery, too, had had to sleep out, to be near their guns and horses, and were in a bad temper.

One young artillery officer was very sarcastic about the mystery which was being made of our movements—the marching by night and hiding by day with no hint as to destination—and said several unflattering things about red tape, brass hat rims, and other insignia of staff. He was an amusing fellow with his wit sharpened to the point of acidity by the cold cheeriest night he had spent in the open, and I stood listening to him for some time. I could imagine him standing between his section of guns directing their fire in the early days of the retreat, when the enemy pressed on us in their masses and every gun had to fire while there was a man left to work it. He would probably have been very witty and deliberate about the objective of the last shell.

Our second night march was longer than the first, and we covered eighteen miles. We appeared still to be going farther and farther away from the enemy, but at one point, nearing the end of the march, we heard faintly the sound of guns. They were the French guns, we were told, so we gathered that we were somewhere behind the French lines. A long climb down took us to a bridge over a river, guarded by a very bored-looking French reservist who looked at us suspiciously, and was, I felt sure, longing for the excuse for a row with somebody, just to relieve the monotony of life. Crossing the bridge we left the main road short of the town—to the keen disappointment of the men—and turned up what looked like a private drive through woods. After going about a mile and a half we came on a group of buildings which proved to be our destination for the night. It was dark and not easy to see much, and we accepted placidly a staff officer's information that the regiment's billeting area lay on the right side of a small stream.

"You will find a farm—it was all I could do for you, but I expect you will all be able to get into it," he said. Tired and footsore as we were, we felt certain we should be able to fix ourselves up anywhere. The farm comprised three cottages, a large building and a huge hay-stack with a corrugated iron roof. We got most of the men on the hay under the corrugated iron roof. Of course, as soon as they lay down they pulled out cigarettes and pipes for a satisfying smoke after the long march. This made Goyle dance with fury, and he sent me up on top of the stack to have all the cigarettes put out. It seemed hard on the men, but he was quite right, as they would certainly have let the stack on fire.

Having got the men settled I went off to find the officers' quarters. These proved to be the two lower rooms of an empty house. There was no furniture in the house at all, simply a thick layer of straw on the floor! However, it had been a long march, and the straw looked inviting enough. I got my valise off the transport, unrolled it in a comer, took off my boots and coat and slid into my sleeping-bag. Others did the same in different comers of the room. The room was not very well lighted, and one or two late comers, who stepped on people's faces or feet in their efforts to find a corner for themselves, came in for a good deal of abuse. In a quarter of an hour we were all sound asleep.

When we woke in the morning we took stock of our quarters, and found they were not so sumptuous as tired limbs and thankfulness to be able to stretch ourselves out rolled up in blankets had led us to suppose. For by daylight we could see by inscriptions scratched on the walls that the last occupants of the place had been a company of the —th Regiment of Turcos. We had been sleeping in what for a time had been a barrack for native troops. On going outside the building and taking a stroll we discovered a pretty little *château* which the officers of another regiment had annexed for their use. They had all slept in beds, washed in comfort, and were having breakfast on a smooth green lawn, surrounded by flowers. We had nowhere to have breakfast except by the side of a wall outside the Turcos' house, and we felt we had done badly over our billets. However, the etiquette of billeting gave the *château* to the other regiment who had first taken it, and we had to put up with what we had got.

The next night we set out on the march again. The march was twenty miles, and proved a severe task for the men after their long spell in the trenches, coming as it did on top of the eighteen-mile march of the night before. It is always the second or third march which tells most on men, and after the first dozen of our twenty miles they began to fall out, till there was a long string of stragglers behind the brigade. In vain the company officers tried to keep their companies together, nothing could make the weary, footsore men keep their fours. Tired as some of the officers were themselves, it was a heavy strain passing up and down the company, stopping to issue "falling out" tickets and running on to catch up the column again. The hardest task of all fell to the subaltern who was detailed to bring up the rear party, and who was not allowed to come into billets until the last man was in. To this unfortunate officer fell the task of trudging along at half a mile an hour behind a group of dead-tired, limping, footsore men. He got into billets four hours after everybody else.

The officers' billets on this occasion were better than those of the night before, for we found a house which had been used by German officers when the town was in the enemy's hands. The house was large and comfortable, and belonged to the mayor of the town. It had been cleared of all valuables, but whether the mayor had done this himself before his departure, or the German officers had looted the place, I cannot say. From the look of things I should imagine that the mayor had takes away all he could and the Germans anything that was left. They had evidently broken open a writing-desk and some drawers, and scattered the contents all over the place. I was guilty of a little looting on my own account, as I found a tattered paper-covered copy of *Madame Bovary*, and not having finished it when it was time to leave, slipped it in my haversack.

We again spent the day around the billets, and as we had a mail with a sack of parcels sent up with the ration convoy we had plenty to occupy ourselves . On active service washing is not necessarily done before breakfast. It is too elaborate a ceremony to be done in a hurry. First a complete outfit has to be got together; one may have a razor but no shaving-brush, or a piece of soap but no towel, or a hairbrush but no comb; possibly one has nothing at all, in which case one is treated as a general nuisance, and borrows from others with difficulty.

But, as a rule, with a depleted cleaning outfit of, say, a razor, a comb and a bit of sponge, the rest can be collected and spread out on a towel. The toilet is then a leisurely process, after which, feeling very clean and fresh and superior, one strolls across to the mess van in one's shirtsleeves for a glass of vermouth and cigarette. After washing there were the letters brought in by the mail to answer, and then lunch and a couple of hours' sleep.

At dusk we moved off again, this time for a very short march, for four miles brought us to our destination, and we were only moved on a little way in order to make room for other troops following on behind.

A night in the village and off we started once more. At one point we passed our divisional general. From the cheery greeting one of his staff officers gave me I surmised something was on foot, and this conjecture proved right, for on reaching a town ten miles distant our billeting orders were suddenly cancelled, and we were told to go on another four miles and entrain. The remainder of the way led through the forest of Compiègne. It was a bright moonlight night, and the forest by night was incomparably lovely. With moonlight playing quietly through the branches It was hard to believe that the forest had ever held troops creeping from tree-trunk to tree-trunk seeking to take each other's lives. In the earlier days of the war we could imagine rival cavalry patrols stealing quietly towards each other along the grass-turfed, shady side of the broad white road, and many a small, bloody encounter must those old trees have seen.

We came on the siding where we were to entrain in a piece of open common. It took some manipulation to get forty men into each truck, but at last we all settled in, a bugle was blown, and we stole away towards the north.

6

The Move Up (2)

Our train journey did not promise to be a comfortable one. We were three aside on the seats of the first-class carriage and the disposition of legs was not easy. However, we all slept without much difficulty, and for six hours the train rumbled through the night to the accompaniment of snores and grunts. The day broke gloriously, and when we looked out of the windows we found ourselves going through a lovely bit of France. Breakfast was the next question; we had in our ration-box a tin of jam, a loaf and a half of bread, and two tins of sardines, also a packet of cocoa. This last possession did not look as though it was going to be particularly useful, as we had nothing but cold water in our bottles.

We ate the sardines and bread and jam and took one or two unappetizing lips from our water-bottles. Then the train stopped, and looking out of the window I saw one or two men standing beside the engine with canteens in their hands. They handed up their tins to the driver, who filled them with boiling water from an exhaust pipe and they proceeded to make tea. Borrowing a couple of canteens from the next carriage I took the packet of cocoa and followed the men's example, so our breakfast was complete.

About noon we reached our destination, a pretty cathedral town in Northern France. After waiting a little while in a siding we detrained and marched off. The town was evidently not one of those which the Germans had entered, for it looked prosperous and well filled. The same sense of security pervaded the country through which we marched; we were, :n fact, outside the zone of war. After following a straight white road out of the town for some four miles, we came to a village where we were to billet for the night. The village priest came forward to assist us in billeting, and the squire of the place sent over a present of wine for the officers and put up the colonel and adjutant in his house.

The next morning I borrowed a horse and rode in to ——, the town at which we had detrained. I had got from the mess president a list of things wanted for the officers'' mess and proceeded to shop. Two dozen eggs were among the items on the list, and I had an opportunity of buying these from a farm cart in one of the streets leading to the town. A passerby happened to overhear me making the bargain and upbraided the good woman selling me the eggs for charging too high a price. I could not quite follow the conversation, which took place in animated French, but I gathered that to ask a British soldier so much for eggs was no way for an ally to behave to a guest and brother-in-arms, and that the farmer's wife thought that passersby should mind their own business.

This sense of hospitality which the passerby had shown pervaded all my shopping transactions; the tradespeople were all cordial, obliging, and most moderate in their charges.

I lunched at the main hotel of the town, which was filled with all the nondescript and various personages who follow an army; there were gentlemen chauffeurs, Red Cross workers, interpreters, and one or two staff officials. At my table there was a clean-shaven, shrewd-looking man wearing the red tabs of staff, who spoke with a strong cockney accent, and did not give the impression of having been a soldier all his life. He said he was attached to general headquarters as spy officer, that is to say, he was responsible for discovering any espionage which went on in our lines. In civil life he looked as though he might be one of those private inquiry agents who advertise in the columns of the Press that they are ready to undertake divorce, financial, and other investigations of a confidential nature. I dare say this is what he was, and I am sure he was a very capable man for the position he held.

After lunch I had my hair cut and shampooed. It was delightful to sit in a hairdresser's chair again and taste some of the luxuries of civilization. I could not help envying the barber his peaceful occupation, which I dare say he is still pursuing and which I knew he would be doing long after I was out of reach of a machine brush and hair oil; and I thought, too, how much pleasanter it would be to be attached to headquarters staff as an espionage officer and have one's lunch in the restaurant of a hotel instead of eating bully and biscuits and dodging shells in a ditch. However, it was no good reflecting and becoming discontented with one's lot, and after completing my purchases I rode back to the village where the regiment was billeted.

Our last march was the longest of all, as we marched all through the night and did not get into the billets where we were to sleep till dawn the next morning. Evans and I shared a room in a cottage, and after eating some breakfast with some delicious coffee, which the woman the cottage belonged to made us, we flung ourselves down on mattresses on the floor and slept. It was past two when I woke, and I hurried off to the headquarters mess to see if there was any lunch left. Luckily the mess sergeant had kept some of the stew he had made for lunch and heated it up for me. After putting down this and half a bottle of wine, I made my way back to the cottage. A stretch of mossy grass under a shady tree looked inviting, and flinging myself down I was soon asleep again.

Some providence must have been watching over me that day, for I woke just ten minutes before the regiment marched off. No one had been able to find me when the order came to move, and they had decided to go off without me. I was glad I had just woken in time, for an officer does not look at his best chasing after a regiment by himself down a road because he has been asleep.

I joined up the group of officers who were sitting by the mess van making a hasty tea and stuffing their haversacks with biscuits.

"I should advise you to take some food," said the adjutant to me, "this may be your last chance. We are going to march five miles, load up on motor-buses, and the transport is to be left behind."

"*The transport to be left behind?*" someone echoed.

"Yes," the adjutant answered a little grimly. "We're for it again."

When a regiment parts with its transport it generally means it is going to fight. We had been with our transport for so many days now that it came as quite a thrill to hear we were to leave it behind. A feeling half of relief that we were going on with the business and half of apprehension came over me.

We marched for an hour or so; at seven o'clock we reached the point of rendezvous for the motor-buses, a long straight stretch of road running through open country just beyond a village. Just before we got to the point of rendezvous the regiment was divided up into parties of thirty men, and a gap of twenty yards left between each party. We did this on the march so that no time was lost in sorting out the different parties. When the last division had been made and all the proper distances between parties obtained, the leading party halted and the others halted behind. The men were then cleared to the right side of the road so that the fleet of motor-buses could come and each halt opposite its party, load up, and move off again with the whole regiment stowed away in no longer time than it took to load thirty men.

When we got to the rendezvous there were no motor-buses and we had to wait. The nights were turning cold; however, not knowing when the next chance might come, most of the men prepared to sleep. In the rush to get off at the start, I had left my greatcoat with the transport and had only a Burberry and a woollen waistcoat with me. I undid my Burberry, unrolled it, pulled out the waistcoat and put both on. Then I lay down by the side of the road, taking care to have a stout tree between myself and any possible motorcars—a very wise precaution if one is sleeping by the roadside anywhere near the Front—slipped my haversack under my head and went to sleep.

A haversack makes quite a good pillow, and when one is tired any piece of ground, which enables one to lie on one's back and take the weight off one's feet, seems soft, and I was soon asleep. Not for long though, as after half an hour I woke with icy feet. I stamped about to warm them, but the thought of going to sleep again and waking up in another half-hour for the same reason was tiresome, so I cast my eye round in the night for some means of keeping warm. I saw what looked like a stack and going up found it was so. While I was busy pulling hay out of the side to make a bed, the motor-buses arrived, and we proceeded to embark. Having got all the men into my bus I was climbing up by the driver on his seat when he shook his head and pointed to the interior of the vehicle, which was a seething mass of Tommies. I shook my head over this and it looked like an *impasse*, as the other officers were all being made to get inside by the different drivers.

However, a knowledge of French and of the ready response of the Frenchman to geniality saved me. For, while pretending to agree to go inside I stood talking with him while we waited to start, offered him a cigarette, and asked him about his wife and family, with the result that when we did set off he said, "*Montez monsieur*" and made room for me on the seat beside him. He said that every night he was driving troops from one part of the line or another—French troops generally, and it was interesting to hear the way in which the French troops used the motor-buses. The warmth of the engine having reached my feet I fell asleep and nodded and lurched beside him on the seat blissfully unconscious for I don't know how many hours and miles.

Once on the journey we halted for a quarter of an hour in a small village. The driver got off the bus and disappeared. Presently he came back and beckoned to me to come with him. I followed him into a cottage where he and several other drivers had had prepared against their arrival hot coffee and rolls of bread and butter. It was extremely kind of the man to have let me in for this feast, which was quite a private affair, and I have seldom enjoyed a cup of coffee more. On we went again and off I went to sleep once more At last, as day broke, we came to the village where we were to halt, climbed off the buses, and sat down by the roadside watching them roll away the way we had come to get more troops.

As we sat by the roadside we soon saw we were nearing more lively parts, for streams of refugees poured by all the time, flying in front of the advancing Germans who were pouring down in strength after the fall of Antwerp. We sat watching the refugees in silence. So this, then, was the reason for our leaving the Aisne and our long secretive seven days move.

7

Nearing the Firing-Line

"We shall have a scrap today," said the staff captain.

"What makes you think so—heard anything?" I asked.

"No, but it is a Sunday, and a fresh batch of officers has arrived," he answered.

Up till then the worst fights in which the regiment had been engaged had always been on a Sunday or just after fresh officers had arrived with reinforcements. The regiment was, at the moment when the staff captain spoke to me, leading the brigade in column of route along a load which we knew ran in the direction of Germany. More than that we knew nothing. We had been on the move for the last few days. Where to or for what purpose we had no idea. All we knew was that in the middle of one night we had been roused from our billets where we were resting, and marched off in a northerly direction. We had marched by night and rested by day in different villages. Never once was any definite information given us as to what was on foot.

Now, at last, if the staff captain's words were true, the move was coming to an end, and we were going into action. Well, if it had to be it had to be, and I think every man was ready to do what was required of him. The officers and draft who had joined us fresh from England were eager for their chance, but the others who had already had a good measure of fighting, and some of whom had been at Mons and on the Marne and Aisne, had not been sorry for the respite which the past fortnight had given. It had been a rest to be away from the sound of gun and rifle fire and go to sleep knowing the enemy was nowhere near, and that one had anyhow the whole of the next day to live.

However, as we marched along there were certain signs which told us that now this state of peace was over. Refugees began to pass us on the road—old men, farmers, and their wives and serving women.

They looked scared, and had few possessions with them. We gathered from them that the Germans were somewhere ahead, pressing forward in vast numbers. Though we did not know it then, it was one of the fierce thrusts for Calais we were being sent to meet.

Further along we were halted in the straggling street of a town. The halt lasted more than the regulation ten minutes, and as we were wondering what was the cause of the delay a troop of British cavalry clattered through. A subaltern rode at the head of the troop, map in hand, hat jauntily over one ear. Presently the remainder of a cavalry brigade came by, and we knew then that the enemy must be some-where near and that the cavalry were being sent out to get in touch with them. They made a brave sight, those cavalrymen, clattering out to pave the way for the infantry and I could not help envying them the excitement and uncertainty of their job.

By the time we advanced the enemy's position would be known and we should be just pawns pushed out at the will of a general to be taken or take.

When the cavalry had gone by we continued our march until we reached a point which was evidently as far as we were to go that evening. Here the colonel sent for officers commanding companies and told them that his orders were to put out two companies on out-post duty along the bank of a canal and keep two in reserve with him in a farm building. It was the lot of my company to be one of the two on outpost duty.

Going out on outpost duty in the middle of a march is one of the hardest lots that can fall on an infantryman. It means that instead of being able to take his boots off, soap his feet (if they are sore), change his sock, have a dinner of hot stew and a good cup of strong tea, he has to spend the night out in the cold watching over the safety of those who are doing these delightful things. He may get a bit of sleep if he is not on group sentry, but it won't be with the same sense of security, and he must lie down in his heavy equipment and have his rifle under his arm.

Off we started with a regretful glance at the farm and others going to billet there in a cosy barn and cook themselves dinner at the kitch-en fire. We soon came to the canal which was to form our outpost line. It lay about half a mile away and looked a very good object to have between ourselves and the enemy. There was one bridge, at which Goyle placed his Maxim. The men he lined along a bank about ten feet high which ran above the tow-path on our side of the canal. This

164

bank proved a blessing m many ways. It saved the men the trouble of entrenching—one of the most irksome items of outpost duty after a long day's march—and provided cover behind which they could walk about, and even enabled them with great care to light small fires to cook tea over until darkness set in. But the bank might also—as Goyle, who had had experience of canal banks at Mons, pointed out—prove a death-trap in the morning, for it would provide a fine mark for the enemy's guns should they get on to it. He therefore insisted on each man scraping himself a small bomb-proof shelter from under the bank.

By great good fortune, just behind the section for which my platoon was responsible there was a cottage. The owners, an old man and his wife, came to the door when I knocked. Like so many of the French peasants they preferred to remain in their home in spite of the proximity of war. They were quite pleased to see Evans, my fellow-subaltern, and myself, and the old woman made us some most delicious coffee, boiled us four eggs, and gave us a loaf of bread. She was delighted with the five francs we were able to scrape up, and promised to get us breakfast in the morning.

It was dark when we had finished, and after a look along the lines, I rolled myself up in a quilt, which I had borrowed from the cottage, and with some straw under me went sound asleep on top of the bank. Not a shot was fired during the night or at dawn to disturb us, so that that night on outpost duty was one of unusual peace and comfort.

In the morning we packed up and continued our march. As we marched in fours along the road, I gathered that my suspicion that there had been really nothing in front of us was correct. A mile or two from the canal a regiment of *spahis* passed us. Incredible as it may seem, these fine little fellows go to war in the scarlet cloaks in which they are dressed in time of peace. They are the most picturesque troops I have ever seen, with their mettlesome Arab horses, turbans, and sweeping scarlet cloaks fastened across the breast high up to the chin.

Farther on we passed a more forceful sight of war. It was a tiny cavalry ambulance convoy. Just one hooded Red Cross wagon driven by a blue-coated cavalryman and followed by a *cuirassier* with bandaged head riding one horse and leading another with an empty saddle. What a picture that little convoy would have made if some artist could have caught it—the pathetic little wagon with its hidden load of pain, the charger and empty saddle, and the splendid *cuirassier* with the bandaged head sitting his horse for all the world to see, proud as a lover who has fought for his mistress.

A mile more and our march was done. We were halted by a way-side inn and told to eat our rations. I went into the inn to see if there was any prospect of a drink, but they were sold out of everything except coffee. That day was probably the briskest day's trade the little inn ever did, and looking at it now it seems odd that the landlady and her daughter should have been bustling about intent solely on business within what proved to be actually half a mile of the firing-line. Two hours later our guns were opening fire in a field by the inn on some Germans in the next village.

As we sat there we now saw two regiments of *cuirassiers* retiring over the open ground towards us. They were part of a French cavalry division which had been lent to cooperate with the British. Magnificent-looking fellows they were, too, with their breastplates and long black plumes; the officers actually had their breastplates burnished, and looked just like our Life Guards at Whitehall.

When we had eaten our rations we fell in again and moved off, and a few hundred yards down the road came on our cavalry, dismounted behind some buildings. From them we learnt that the enemy had been located about half a mile farther down the road. We were told from this point to leave the road and move in sections across country, and in this formation passed on beyond the cavalry. They had done their job and found the enemy, and it was now for us to come and take up the line.

8

Getting Into Action

After the cavalry had withdrawn my regiment was lined out along a road running at right angles to the road down which we had advanced. From this time onwards for the next ten days I only knew what the companies on my left and right were doing, and not always that. As a platoon commander, I was responsible for the fifty men under me, and all the information it was necessary for me to have was included in the orders which Goyle, my company commander, gave for the movements of my platoon. Therefore, for general knowledge of the battle, I had to rely on such deductions as I could make from sound of firing on my right and left and any gossip I could pick up when I went back to regimental headquarters.

Advancing to attack in these days of modern warfare is a very slow business. It is essential that platoons, companies, and regiments should move forward together in one line and not allow gaps to come between them, and what with one regiment waiting for another to advance, and each waiting for orders from their respective colonels, who in turn are waiting for the word from the brigadier, there is often considerable delay. This delay is to a certain extent mitigated by the general policy of junior officers of pushing forward on their own initiative until they are stopped.

As a platoon commander one works with the platoon commander on one's left or right, leaving the platoon sergeant to keep in touch with the platoon on the other flank. To have a fellow subaltern to talk to as one lies in a ditch being shelled is a great comfort.

However, we were kept along the road we had first lined for about an hour before any further move was made, and most of the officers of the regiment congregated in a little group while we were waiting for orders. I was much interested in watching the doings of some gunner officers who had come up. Two of them were surveying the ground in front through field-glasses. From where we were we could see nothing, and as there had not been a shot fired that day we did not know how many of the enemy there were in front of us or where they were. However, the gunners were able to see something, for, after a bit, they conferred with the battery commander. Acting on their information he sent back a message for the guns to come up, and up they dashed, wheeled into line in the field, and unlimbered.

I happened to be standing near the battery commander, and ventured to ask him what he was going to do.

"I'm going to shell ——ville," he replied.

He was a squat, stumpy little major, who looked as though he had just made a capital breakfast, and he spoke of his intentions with as much complacency as if he was going out for a morning's partridge-shooting. Two minutes later he had given a crisp order, and the six businesslike grey nozzles had barked in sharp succession, and sent six shells screaming over the quiet countryside. Poor ——ville! Many shells have since crashed into the pretty little French village, but I shall never forget seeing its baptism of fire or the complacent way in which the tubby little major announced that he was going to shell the place.

Soon after this orders came for the infantry to advance, and Goyle sent for his four platoon commanders and gave his orders. Our company was responsible for keeping touch with the Dorchester Regiment on our left; No. 5 platoon, under Evans, was immediately responsible for this, with No 6 (mine) next, and 7 (under Edwards), and 8 (under Mayne), on the right. This was to be the first day's fighting for Edwards and Mayne, as they had only come out from England with reinforcements two days before. Edwards had been a Sandhurst cadet a month ago, but Mayne was a retired officer who had fought in South Africa; however, there was nothing to choose in composure between the boy and the man.

Goyle took us to a point where we could see the ground we were to move over, and showed us a ditch which he wished us to crawl along until we reached another ditch at right angles to it which we were to line. In this way we should be able to do the first part of the advance without being seen at all. Evans took his platoon out first, and when he had got a good start I followed with mine. He reached the ditch without mishap, but here we had to remain some while, as the Dorchester Regiment on our left had not got up in line with us.

Verbal messages then passed between Evans and the subaltern in command of the right platoon of the Dorchester Regiment. Evans wanted to know why the Dorchesters were not in line with him, and the subaltern of the Dorchester's why he, Evans, had advanced so far. Up till now our guns behind had been firing steadily over our heads, and not a sound or sign had come from the enemy, but now suddenly, in the middle of the argument between Evans and the Dorchester subaltern, there was a different whistle in the air, a crash, and a white puff of smoke just behind us.

"Hullo!" Evans looked round and slid quickly to the bottom of the ditch.

The enemy's first shell was followed by two others, which burst about the same place, and then by three which fell farther over us.

"They are after our guns," said Evans.

This was my first taste of hostile shell-fire, but the shells passed so harmlessly overhead that it hardly seemed as though we were under fire at all. After a while orders came for us to continue our advance. This time my platoon had to lead the way and advance up a ditch to another parallel ditch about three hundred yards away. We gained the ditch without incident, but it was a queer experience, pushing forward over the empty fields, never knowing when we were coming on the enemy or what lay ahead of us. When my platoon and the platoon under Evans were safely in the ditch, No. 7 was told to follow. To reach our line No. 7 had to cross over some open ground, and this proved their undoing, for midway across a shell burst just in front of them, followed by another and another.

"By Jove," said Evans, "Edward's lot has been spotted."

We watched. Edwards, as soon as he came under fire, had halted his men beneath a bit of bank, and from where we were we could see no sign of a man above the surface of the ground. But the enemy battery had evidently found their mark, for they plastered the little bank with shrapnel. I watched, able to do nothing and sorry in my heart. It was a very fierce baptism of fire for a Sandhurst cadet, and I wondered how the boy was faring.

It was now well on towards dusk, and as the light failed the firing stopped. Slowly, what was left of the exposed platoon began to creep up to our ditch, and much to my delight Edwards himself came up unhurt with the first man. He said he had had ten men hit, a man sitting beside him killed, and a tree just above blown in half,. The boy seemed none the worse for his experience, and only a little anxious lest he had exposed his men unnecessarily to fire.

It now looked as though we were to spend the night where we were. I posted a patrol out in some bushes ahead and told the men to get to work with their entrenching tools to improve their cover. As it grew darker, the strain of looking out into the night for an enemy who never appeared became oppressive. Evans reported from the left that he could see no sign of the Dorchester Regiment, and we appeared to be in rather an isolated position. Much to my relief Goyle came up soon and said he intended to withdraw the company to the place whence we had started. It was a great relief to be able to lie down close to our own guns and near the colonel and regimental headquarters.

As soon as the men were settled I went back to the first-line transport to get the officers" rations for the next day. Goyle had given me the job of feeding the five officers in the company, leaving it to me to make arrangements for cooking where possible, and, when not, to see that each had a parcel of food to last him through the day. I found the regimental quartermaster-sergeant busy issuing rations to the different company orderly corporals. The work was being done in a barn by the light of a guttering candle. In a corner of the barn five of Edwards's platoon, who had come under the shrapnel fire, lay stretched out stiff and cold.

The quartermaster-sergeant saluted me cheerily and packed my ration-box with our rations, giving me a piece of bacon to divide between us, a wedge of cheese, fifteen army biscuits, a tin of jam, and three small tins of bully beef. With the box under one arm I started back for the company. On the way, having learnt from a sentry where regimental headquarters were, I just peeped in to see what was going on. After the day's work, there is often something to be picked up at regimental headquarters in the way of a tot of whisky from a bottle sent down by the Brigadier, or a helping from a dixie of soup sent up by the master-cook. Young subalterns are not supposed to hang about waiting for these delicacies, but if they do push a hungry face round the door and hastily withdraw it a kindly colonel or adjutant will often ask them in. Having therefore located regimental headquarters as being in the kitchen of a farm, I tapped on the door and asked if anyone had seen Goyle.

"Yes," here he is, said the colonel, and I saw my company commander's nose emerge from a steaming cup of coffee. Round the fire were the colonel, adjutant, scout and machine-gun officers, the doctor, Goyle, and two other company commanders. These little informal gatherings are held by most regiments when the day's work is done and the night is not going to be busy, and a great relief it is, too, to be able to laugh and see the funny side of things after the strain of an anxious day. At the first sound of firing they melt.

I was given a cup of coffee and wheedled a cigarette out of a scout officer, who had just had some sent out from England. After warming myself for a quarter of an hour I said goodnight and returned to the company across the field, taking with me a bundle of straw from the farmyard, which made a capital bed.

9

An Attack at Dawn

I had not been sleeping long when I was awakened by a foot gently feeling the small of my back.

Looking up, I saw Evans standing over me.

"Goyle wants you," he said; "he is just dawn there." Evans pointed to a dark corner of the ditch in which the company was spending the night.

I got up from the pile of straw on which I was lying and followed him. Goyle was squatting on the ground with a map and an electric torch which he was shading under his greatcoat. He had just come back from battalion headquarters, where he had been to receive orders.

"We are going to attack at dawn," he began, as soon as his four platoon commanders were settled round him. "We are to gain the line——," he indicated the points on the map which marked the position we were to capture. "The Dorchesters have orders to take ——ville"—he pointed to a village on our left—"and the ——th Brigade are to take ——"—he pointed to another village marked on the right. "The attack begins as soon as it is light, which will be 5 a.m. I want you to see now that the platoons return their tools" (we had been digging earlier in the night), "that each man has his rations, and that twenty-five *bandoliers* of spare ammunition are carried per platoon. The mist will cover the first part of our advance, and there must be no firing until the order is given by me."

We went off to carry out the instructions given, and then lay down to wait for the dawn.

Perhaps Evans and the other platoon commanders slept. I don't know. I know only that for my part I did not. The thought that we were to attack at dawn dispelled any lingering sleepiness. I looked at my watch—3 a.m.—in an hour it would begin to grow light. How would the day end? What would be the fate of the attack? I wondered if Goyle was awake, and thought I would go down to him. I peeped down into the corner of the ditch where I knew he was lying. A dark form lay stretched at full length, and I heard a gentle snore. I lay down again.

After a while looking out in the direction of the enemy, I saw a faint flush low in the sky. I watched. The flush swelled to a vast crimson glow. I woke Goyle. For a moment we looked at the day breaking blood-red over the fields across which we were to fight our way. Then we went, one either way along the ditch, rousing the men.

The men yawned, stretched themselves, and stood to arms. Their bayonets, which they always kept firmly fixed during the night, glittered faintly in the early light. The crimson flush was broken now, and streaks of yellow and pure white shot across the sky.

Goyle caught my arm.

Low on the horizon the crest of a yellow ball just showed above the trees. "The sun," he said.

CRASH! Bang! CRASH! Bang! Bang! Bang!

We listened as our guns behind opened the ceremony with a salvo. They fired fast for five or ten minutes.

"The Dorchesters are advancing on our left, sir"—the message was passed down to Goyle.

He signed for the company to advance. The men crawled up out of the ditch and pushed over the country in a thin line. Evans was on my left, with Edwards and No. 8 platoon commander on the right.

We advanced very slowly, with long pauses, lying flat on the ground waiting for orders to continue. Now the officer commanding the company on the right would send word to say he had reached such a point, and would C Company come up in line with him? Now Evans passed along that we were getting ahead of the Dorchesters. The attack is a very slow and ticklish business in these days of modern firearms. All this while steady firing could be heard on the right as the —th Brigade swung round, and for about an hour there was sharp firing on the left, but in front of us not a shot was heard.

At last we gained a group of cottages on a road which marked the point we had been told to reach. There was still no sign of the enemy, and had it not been for the firing on the right and left we should have doubted his existence in the neighbourhood, so quiet and peaceful did the cottages look.

However, we heard afterwards that the brigade on the right had suffered heavily, and that the brisk firing on the left was the Dorchester Regiment under machine-gun fire from the village they had been told to take. It just happened to be our luck that day to have an uncontested piece of frontage to advance over.

A road ran through the group of houses and beyond a ploughed field. At the end of the ploughed field there was a hedge and ditch which formed a natural trench facing the enemy. In spite of the apparent absence of the enemy Goyle refused to allow the men to loiter about along the road or in the farms and cottages, but ordered the company to line this ditch. As it turned out later it was well he did so.

As soon as I had seen my platoon lined along their section of the ditch I went back to a farm behind to explore. I found Jenkins, my soldier servant, there before me, busy searching the farm for breakfast. He had found half a dozen new-laid eggs in an outhouse, kindled a small fire in the farmyard, and was boiling the eggs in his canteen. He was not, strictly speaking, supposed to be doing this, but soldier servants are a privileged class, and Jenkins was the most tactful of servants. On my going up to him to see what he was doing he pointed to the eggs triumphantly and said they were for me. So instead of telling him to join the company at once in the ditch I stayed with him to watch them boil. I had not been in the farmyard two minutes when suddenly sharp firing broke out from the ditch. So we had found something in front of us at last.

I dashed across the ploughed field to my platoon, leaving Jenkins, quite unperturbed, still watching the eggs. Reaching the ditch I flung myself down beside Evans, who was lying against the bank peering to the front through the hedge. We could see nothing; however, our fellows continued to fire furiously. For the first minute or two the firing was so hot that both Evans and I thought there must be something ahead of us. As it continued, though we could still see nothing, we crept along behind the men to try to find out what they were firing at. My platoon sergeant informed me that he thought the enemy were lining the corner of a wood 400 yards away. He had seen one or two dodging in and out among the trees. However, as no reply was made to our fire, I ordered that no man was to fire unless he saw something, and gradually the line grew quiet again.

Suddenly there was a dull report from a distant point in front, and a shell whistled overhead. Looking back, I saw it strike the roof of the farm where I had left Jenkins. Poor Jenkins! I wondered if he was still cooking those eggs! However, I had no time to speculate on his fate, for the enemy, having located our position owing to our own rather unnecessarily aggressive outburst of rifle fire, began to shell us. Round after round they sent crashing into the cottages and farms, and then, shortening their range, began to put shots just over our ditch. Well it was that Matley had made all the men get into the ditch from the beginning. It was a fine deep ditch, and few of the many thousands of shrapnel bullets found their mark.

Soon after the shelling started it began to rain heavily. It was a weird experience lying there in the ditch with the rain pouring down on us from above and the shrapnel bullets crashing sideways like a leaden hailstorm through the hedge. The men pulled their waterproof sheets from their packs, and, spreading these over themselves, lay down in the ditch, smoking unconcernedly. Now and again a wounded man whose cover had not been sufficient would crawl by. One very fat lance-corporal I remember, puffing along on his hands and knees as fast as his rifle and pack would let him. He kept slipping, catching his pack in the branches, and swearing profusely. He had been caught in the most fleshy part of his body, and evidently was of the opinion that there was no place like home, for from time to time he grunted, "Stretcher bearer! Stretcher bearer! 'Ere! I've been 'it!" He was a most comic sight, and I couldn't help laughing as he passed.

The firing went on intermittently throughout the day. At dusk we were withdrawn, another company taking our place in the ditch. We were formed up behind the shelter of a farm wall on the road behind, and told we were going to be taken back into reserve for the night.

By the farm I found Mulligan, a brother subaltern. Taking me gently by the elbow he led me into the farm kitchen, through a door beyond, and down some cellar steps. I lit my torch to look around. The cellar floor was heaped with broken and empty bottles and corks. On a shelf were half-finished glasses of wine. A party of German soldiers had evidently been in before us and helped themselves, breaking what they could not drink. However, they had left one or two bottles intact amid the debris, from which Mulligan and I each had a good glass of red wine, for which I hope the owner, if he ever returns to his battered home, will forgive us.

Coming out of the farm, much to my delight, I met Jenkins still alive, in spite of the shell-fire. He pressed two cold, hard objects into my hand.

"How did you get these?" I asked.

"They were them eggs I was cooking this morning," he replied; "I had to quit when that first shell came—nearly went up, eggs and all, with it. But I went back afterwards. The fire was out—but they was boiled all right, if you don't mind 'em hard."

10

The Reserve Company

After D Company had taken over our section of trench we remained on the road behind for a time, while the authorities were deciding what to do with us. Goyle said the question was whether we were required to fill a gap between our right company and the Dorchesters on our left or whether our right company and the Dorchesters between them could span this gap and enable us to go back as reserve company into billets.

We waited in the rain for our orders. The men stood expectantly with their rifles slung over their shoulders, their hands in their pockets, and their greatcoat collars turned up to their ears. They said little. Now and again one would say to another hopefully, "We're going back to billets—ain't we, Bill?" One or two of my N.C.O.s came up and asked me if I knew what was going to happen, and I told them the situation, about which, like the dutiful fellows they were, they expressed no opinion. He is a wonderful fellow on active service it Tommy Atkins. However roughly his inclinations may be torn he never says a word, but just does what it required of him so long as he can stand. Those men would have gone off to fill the gap that night without a question or thought except that it had to be done, and perhaps a "Gor blimey!" on life in general and European warfare in particular.

However, it was to be billets that night. Goyle came up with the order from battalion headquarters. The company fell-in in fours and marched down the road. I don't know what it is, but there is a sort of feeling about a body of men marching which conveys a lot to a trained ear. In the ready click of the rifle to the shoulder and the steady tramp of the fifty pairs of feet behind me I could read hearts full of thankfulness as we headed down the lane towards the tiny village where we were to billet.

It was by now nearly ten o'clock. The village itself consisted of two farms and half a dozen cottages, and the adjutant was disposed to say that it was hardly worth billeting the men in view of the lateness of the hour and the possibility of their having to turn out at short notice. He suggested they should lie down in a field. However, Evans and I guaranteed to have all the men in billets within a quarter of an hour and to make ourselves personally responsible for knowing where they all were and turning them out at short notice if required. The adjutant, who was merely taking up the point of view proper to adjutants of not wanting to run the risk of any company being caught napping, was agreeable to this, and off we started.

To be able to billet a company quickly is a question of practice. The eye quickly gets trained to know what amount of men will go into what space and the look of likely places. To stow away 200 men in a tiny village of two farms and four cottages would at first seem a difficult task, especially when a certain amount of the space has already been taken up by different details attached to battalion headquarters. Barns are the first things to look for, and we were lucky in finding two, which each held fifty men. The French barns always have plenty of straw in them, and make warm, snug lying.

An empty stable took another fifty men, and an outhouse twenty-five; the remaining twenty-five had to be content with a sort of porch which ran long a wall. These last we were subsequently able to transfer to the barn on finding there would just be room for them. The process of billeting the men did not take more than the quarter of an hour we had estimated, one of us going ahead to explore, the other following with the men and standing at the entrance to the barn or outhouse, counting them in and flashing his torch into the interior to show the way.

Having got the men under cover, we looked about for a place for ourselves. Goyle had been offered a mattress in the kitchen of the farm where the colonel and adjutant were making their battalion headquarters. He was also no doubt going to have some of the colonel's supper, and might be considered arranged for for the night. But there was no room for four hungry subalterns at battalion headquarters. We had received our day's rations and were expected to look after ourselves. Four sergeants were using the kitchen of the other farm, and of the cottages only one, from a light in the window, looked as though it was inhabited. Evans and I pushed our way into this but found the kitchen already occupied. Six Tommies were sitting round the stove watching a stew simmer in a pan. They did not belong to our company, but were some of the headquarters details. The cottage was certainly theirs by right of annexation, and Evans and I turned to go out.

"Beg pardin, sir," said one of the men; "but there's another room at the back." This was extremely kind and hospitable of the man, as the little class distinctions between officer and man are to a certain extent preserved on active service, and the Tommy who has found a nook likes to keep it to himself just as much as the officer.

Evans and I accepted the invitation and went to inspect the other room. We found a comfortable cottage bedroom with two large four-post beds. The old woman to whom the cottage belonged and her husband said we were welcome to the use of the beds, and the sight of them was so tempting that I am afraid we did not trouble to inquire where she and her old man would sleep.

Jenkins, my servant, and the other two platoon commanders being then found, we put a stew of bully beef and vegetables on the fire, and, having eaten this, doubled up on the two beds.

Impossible to describe the joy of throwing off our wet boots and coats, stretching ourselves on the mattresses, and pulling a blanket up to our chins. We were soon all fast asleep.

After six hours real rest we woke feeling fit for anything. When we went out into the lane we found Jenkins in the middle of preparations for breakfast. He had dragged a table outside the cottage, discovered two chairs and two packing-cases, and laid four places with a miscellaneous assortment of knives and forks. For breakfast we had some fried ration bacon, a small and carefully apportioned wedge of bread each from the only loaf to be found in the village, coffee, and a tin of marmalade.

The company passed the day in converting a ditch into a trench. Although they were supposed to be resting in reserve, the men needed no urging to dig. The day before they had come under shrapnel fire when they were fortunately in a fine natural trench, but the memory of the murderous hail of bullets which had swept over their heads was sufficiently vivid to make them all anxious to provide themselves with equally good cover against a second attack. Each man worked away individually for himself, digging away into and under the ground until he had scooped a little burrow in which he would be secure from shrapnel, no matter how accurately it burst over the trench. As the men finished their burrows to their satisfaction they lay down in them, pulled out their pipes and cigarettes, and smoked, watching with complacent interest the efforts of neighbours who had roots or rocks or other difficulties in the soil to contend with.

The morning passed quietly, but at noon the enemy sent several shells over the ground where we were. One of these shells struck one of the cottages, crumpling it like a matchbox. I happened at the time to be back in the cottage where we had slept, helping Jenkins to concoct a stew for lunch. It was pitiful to see the terror of the old peasant woman and her husband, who sat dumbly in their kitchen, waiting for one of the great projectiles to come and wreck their home. As each shell fell the old woman lifted her hands and gave a little pitiful gasp. It was all more than she could understand, and no efforts of Jenkins or myself could calm her.

However, they were a brave old couple, and as soon as the shelling was over busied themselves getting us potatoes and carrots for our stew from a store they had in a loft. They were delighted with a tin of army bully beef which we gave them for themselves. Except for this old couple, the farms and cottages were deserted, and I rather wondered why they had remained. Probably because they were too frightened and bewildered to do anything else.

Just before dusk we heard the dull report of a heavy gun in the distance. *R-rump—CRASH*—a shell burst a quarter of a mile to our right. Again the gun boomed, and again the dull "*R-rump*," followed by a loud explosion and cloud of mud and earth in the same place. The men stirred uneasily in their dugouts. They knew what it was— 60 lb. high-explosive melinite. It was no joke like shrapnel, this. If the enemy happened to turn a few on to us we should be blown to bits. It was an anxious time listening to the gun and waiting for the shells to explode. But they did not seem to be swinging round in our direction, and darkness found us all still safe. At eight the order came for the company to go back into the firing-line.

11

A Night Attack

After twenty-four hours in reserve it was our turn to go back into the firing-line and relieve A Company. We took over A Company's trenches at dusk, Goyle going with each platoon commander, showing him his section, and giving orders about the posting of groups and improvement of cover.

My section of trench had already been worked on by the company we took over from. The officer before me had scooped out a dug-out for himself at one end and lined it with straw. This I marked off for my own use, and then went along the line to see that all the men were busy. By the time I had inspected the trench and put out an advanced post it was quite dark, and I settled myself down in my own dugout with a pious hope that the night would remain fine and we should all be able to pass it comfortably. There was no sound from the front, and it looked as though we should be undisturbed.

One by one the stars came out, the night grew colder, and I pulled on my greatcoat. It was weird lying there in the darkness, hearing nothing, seeing nothing, with only the dark shapes of the men on each side and the occasional tinkle of an entrenching tool against a stone to remind one that one was taking part in a great war. I wondered what my friends at home were doing, thought of dances at the Ritz and the happy days when one dressed for dinner, and smiled to think what a funny sight I must look tucked up for the night in a ditch.

As I lay there I heard far away on the right the sound of rifle fire. Were they our troops or the French? Perhaps it was one of our divisions which we had been told was swinging round on our flank. So the division had done its march and was fighting now. I was glad we were not. It was much better to lie peacefully in a ditch. Fighting meant seeing one's pals killed—crawling about, peering forward with tired eyes—worry, anxiety, with, of course, always the fever of excitement. But we had all had a full share of excitement, and were not sorry to lie still until we were wanted. Hullo! The sound of firing was drawing nearer and swelling in volume. That must be the brigade on our right engaged. Ah! There were two sharp shots from the farm where the next company lay.

"Pass along the word for every man to stand to," I called, jumping to my feet.

"Sergeant X," I said to the N.C.O. next to me, "go down the trench and see that every man is awake."

Pht! pht! pht!

I ducked down into the trench. Half a dozen bullets came singing through the edge. There was sharp firing now on our right. The next company was evidently engaged. Away beyond the rifle fire had swelled into one big crash of sound. Suddenly a hot fire broke out in front of us. To the left I heard our two Maxims, like watchdogs, barking viciously. It was a night attack, then—the enemy had come up to have a go at us.

"Quick—get into the trench and line along to your left. Where do you want me"

I looked up and saw Mulligan hurrying his men into my trench. He had been sent up with his platoon from the reserve company to strengthen the line.

"Anywhere you like, old boy," I called back; "but I should get down out of that quick." The bullets were literally singing round him.

Our men were now all standing up to the parapet, firing into the night. I craned forward, trying to see in the darkness. A bullet lopped a branch off my ear, and I withdrew my head hurriedly.

"They're all awake, sir," said Sergeant X, as he returned to his place beside me.

"So it seems," I answered, as the din from our rifles swelled into a deafening volume. "Here, mind where you are pointing that gun," I said to the man on my left, as he brought down a bit of the hedge in front of my nose in his effort to get off five rounds in as many seconds.

"No. 5 platoon are running short of ammunition," the word came down the trench.

"Tell No. 6 to pass along any they have to spare and save their fire as much as possible," I ordered.

It was going to be a tight business this, with the enemy's fire growing hotter every minute and our ammunition supply running short.

Again the message came down, "No. 5 platoon are running short of ammunition."

I looked at Sergeant X. We had already sent men back for fresh supplies. "I'll go back, sir," said Sergeant X. It seemed impossible for him to get out of the trench and cross the bullet-swept open ground. Still, it was the only thing to be done. I nodded.

Grasping his rifle, he turned to clamber out of the trench. Just as he was going a voice from behind called, "Where will you have this sir"

There was a thump behind, and two men rolled over into the trench dragging a box of ammunition after them. They sat up and mopped their foreheads. "Lord! it's like hail out there," said one of them breathlessly, "and that stuff weighs about a ton," pointing to the box of ammunition.

"Well, come on, mate," and back they went out of the trench to the rear for more.

Sergeant X and I wrenched the lid off the box of ammunition and started passing the *bandoliers* down the trench.

"Pass these right along to No. 5 platoon," I ordered.

A second box was brought up by two more panting men. I distributed the contents among my own platoon. This put a better complexion on things. With plenty of ammunition we had nothing to fear, but the anxiety had been great. The sensation of running short of water in the desert is as nothing compared to that of running short of ammunition in action.

"They're getting closer, aren't they? "I said to Sergeant X, listening to the enemy's fire.

"I think they are, sir." He refilled his magazine and bent once more over the rifle.

"By gad! did you see that flash—they are only a hundred yards off. Here, give me that." I took the rifle from a man next me who had been wounded, and laid it, with the bayonet fixed, on the parapet in front. At the same time I drew my revolver and put it ready for use by my other hand. It was getting exciting this—quite pleasantly so.

"What do we do if they charge—get out and meet 'em?" I asked. My sergeant had had more experience of action than I, and I felt I could well afford to ask his advice.

"Just stay where we are, sir," he answered; but they won't do that; they don't like these"—he tapped his bayonet. He was a splendidly calm fellow, that sergeant, and it was good to feel him firm as a rock beside me. All men, N.C.O.S, officers, and privates, instinctively lean towards each other when the corner is tight.

For the next five hours the firing continued, sometimes dying down, sometimes swelling to a sharp volley. Ammunition boxes arrived and were emptied. There were moments of acute anxiety when the supply seemed running short. Each man was told to keep fifteen rounds by him at all costs to meet a charge. Sergeant X bent steadily over his rifle, pumping lead into the dark patch where the enemy appeared to be. Sometimes I could hear guttural voices and harsh words of command, somewhere away there in the blackness the enemy were lying. I could see clearly for about forty yards. Would masses of dark shapes suddenly appear? They should have ten rounds from the rifle, then six from the revolver, and then the bayonet would be left. Furtively under cover of the parapet I lit a cigarette, and holding it well screened from the front, puffed big satisfying gasps. All the while the rifles rattled like the sharp ticking of a clock.

The firing grew quieter, and from the front there was now only an occasional shot. I suddenly felt sleepy, as though lulled by the rattle of the rifle fire. I sat down a moment on the edge of my dugout.

"Mr. Mulligan's compliments, and could you tell him the time, sir?" I pulled myself together with a start.

By Jove, I had nearly been asleep. "What's the time, sergeant?" I asked. There was no reply. Sergeant X was nodding as he stood, arms folded over his rifle. He, too, as the firing died down had been overcome by sleep. I sent back the rime to Mulligan, each man passing the message to the man next him.

"Mr. Mulligan's compliments, and would you like a biscuit, sir?" A biscuit was pressed into my hand which had come the same way as the message.

"Mr ——'s compliments to Mr. Mulligan, and would he care for a piece of cheese?" I wrapped a piece of cheese in a piece of paper and sent it back.

So we kept passing messages to one another all through the night, and no man slept. With the enemy a hundred yards away it was advisable they should not; but, like Sergeant X and myself, each, once the fierce strain of firing had passed, found the inclination well-nigh irresistible.

At last the dawn broke, and we saw the ground clear in front of us.

12

The Farm in the Firing-Line

A farm lay behind our trench. Just in front of the farm there ran a wooden fence. This fence had been loopholed and banked with earth, and was now held by a platoon of infantry. Trenches ran to the right and left in continuation of the fence, and were manned by the remaining platoons of the company. For two days now the enemy had attacked the farm, and all through the past night bullets had come smack-smack against the walls, like heavy hailstones. It was a fair-sized farm built round a yard, three sides grain lofts and cattle sheds and the remaining side a dwelling-place. The company commander, the company sergeant-major, the stretcher-bearers, and others who were attached to company headquarters were standing about in the yard. One or two of the men had their coats off and were shaving and washing in buckets of water. As there had been no firing since dawn, and the enemy had evidently withdrawn after their unsuccessful attack during the night, Evans and I left our platoons and came into the farm..

Goyle, like the wise company commander he was, made no comment on our having left our trenches, relying on us to know when we ought to go back, and said that there was a room in the farm which the farmer's wife had jet apart for the officers, and that we should find some food inside. This room, which was evidently the best parlour, was approached through the kitchen which opened on the front door.

Never shall I forget the sight as I opened the front door and looked into the kitchen. The small stone-flagged room was filled with civilians. These were evidently peasants from outlying cottages who had left their homes when the fighting began and flocked to the farm as a central place of refuge. At a wooden table sat a party of four women, two with children. One woman was weeping bitterly. The others were trying to console her. All were drinking from bowls of soup. The

185

farmer's wife was stirring a fresh pot of soup over the stove. She was a fine-looking woman, with proud, sad eyes. Seeing Evans and me standing at the door, she beckoned to us to come in, and gave us each a cup of soup. Beside the stove sat an old, old man, his head resting against his hand, staring fixedly before him.

Sometimes he moaned gently. He sat like this all day, refusing to talk to anybody, or to eat anything, or to be comforted. The farmer's wife told us that the day before a shell had hit his cottage and killed his horse. He was the village carrier. The horse was perhaps as old as himself—as horses' years are measured—still it had been his companion and means of livelihood, and now it was taken from him. He could not understand it all—why the shell had come to wreck his home and kill his horse. He just sat there moaning and staring before him. We turned away. Neither we nor the farmer's wife could do anything. But with the weeping woman at the table it might be different.

The farmer's wife thought that we, being British officers, could do something. She brought the woman up to us and she told us her tale. Her husband, it seemed, had been hit by a bullet while working in his field. He now lay out there wounded. She could not say she was sure if he was dead, but could we go and get him in. They had fired at her when she tried to go out to him. It was terrible to feel he was still lying there. We asked where the field was and then looked at each other helplessly. It lay in no man's land, between ours and the German lines. Perhaps at night, but for the rest of the day, no—we could do nothing.

While we were drinking our soup two more refugees came in: a broken-looking middle-aged peasant, with red-rimmed eyes and thin shambling legs, and his wife. He was clinging round his wife's neck, tears pouring from the red-rimmed eyes. He, too, like the old peasant by the stove, was speechless; his wife told us that the Germans had taken him and made him march in front of them for three days.

She repeated the words "*trois jours*" her voice shaking with passion. The farmer's wife set the couple at the table and gave them soup from the pot. I wondered that she, too, did not join in the general weeping; but she went quietly and sadly about her work, saying little, giving food and drink to the afflicted people who had come to her kitchen, tending her pots and pans and fire. She asked no questions about the enemy, where they were or when we should drive them from the farm. She showed no signs of the night of terror she must have passed as the fight raged about her house. It was as though she stood for the spirit of France, proud to suffer for her country, confident in the prowess of her men, and patient and undoubting that they would succeed.

Later, when Goyle came, she ushered us all into the parlour she had reserved for our use. She watched us for a moment as we opened a tin of bully beef and pulled some biscuits from our pockets, and then, motioning to us to put these things away, began to dust the table and lay a cloth. In a short while she had put before us a dainty lunch, soup, boiled chicken, a stew of vegetables, coffee, and cheese. We would have preferred our servants to have done the cooking and waited on ourselves, so that she could look after her own people, but she insisted on doing everything herself, bringing each dish in. We asked her if we could do anything for her, and she drew up a methodical list of things she wanted from a neighbouring village—coffee, rice, flour, and oil for her lamp. I got up to get these things, and at the door she stopped me and pressed her well-worn purse into my hand to buy the things. I had difficulty in making her take the money back.

Outside the farm I found a party of men burying one of the company who had been killed in the night. They had wrapped him in his coat, and were digging a rough grave by the roadside. One of the men was at work on a wooden cross made of two bits of board from the lid of a ration-box. He had scrawled R.I.P. and the date in large letters, and was laboriously tracing out the dead man's name and number.

The village where I was to get the provisions lay about half a mile away along an open, desolate road. All along the road men lay entrenched. The word had gone round that the enemy had withdrawn, and most of the men were sleeping beside their rifles. Some of the inhabitants of the village were coming back after the attack, and I found a tiny store open where I could get the things the farmer's wife required. On my way back I passed a wine shop, which was crowded with peasants, all talking and drinking coffee and little glasses of rum.

I wondered what they thought of it all, and imagined they were too bewildered to have any opinions. On all their faces were evident signs of satisfaction at being able to return to the village. They thought that the "*boches*" were by now probably running back hard to Germany, and all would be over in a few days.

As I stood in the doorway three civilian youths approached, two of them supporting a third between them. The lad in the middle looked white and scarcely able to stand. I went up to see if I could do anything. The two with him told me that they had found the boy lying in a field; he had been hit in five places by shrapnel. They thought he must have been lying there unattended for three days. The boy himself watched me with dumb, pain-ridden eyes. Very weakly and slowly he raised his hand to his mouth and pointed to his tongue, which was black and swollen. "*Soif*," he whispered.

Of course, he had had no water all the time. I had him taken into a cottage and laid on a table. I got a glass of water from a well and held it to his lips. He was too weak to raise his head, but his friends supported him, and he drank the water slowly and steadily. As he drank a little smile played about his lips, and when the glass was empty, before they laid him down, he nodded his head and smiled at me as only those smile for whom one has done some last service and whose life is nearly done.

I made my way back to the farm with sickness in my heart. Not all the fighting nor the strain of war had affected me as the sight of those suffering, helpless people whose ground we were using for our battlefield.

That night we said goodbye to the farmer's wife and pushed on beyond the farm. We were all happy to feel we were leaving her behind the security of our lines. As she stood at the door and watched us go there was still the same look in her eyes as when we came—a look of sadness, resignation, and infinite courage.

13

Pushing Forward

An hour before dawn the men stood to their arms in the trenches, but as the daylight grew and there was no sound or sight of the enemy, first one man and then another got out of the trench. These being allowed to walk about with impunity the others soon followed their example. Fires were lit for cooking, and men spread themselves on the ground behind the trench reading old copies of newspapers, or mending their clothes, or cleaning their rifles. Here and there parties could be seen carrying away corpses which had been stiff and cold behind the trench for the last forty-eight hours. Goyle, my company commander, walked across from his headquarters. The day before it had been impossible for him to get to us, and messages were brought by orderlies, who crawled up on their stomachs along a narrow ditch.

"Morning," said Goyle; "looks as though they had cleared."

"Yes, sir," I answered, "there has been no sign of anything ahead this morning."

"I reckon that was their transport we heard, sir—they was rumbling along a road there, sir, all the night," said my platoon-sergeant.

The man was probably right, for all through the night a rumbling of wagons had been plainly audible along a road behind the enemy's lines. The night before we had been attacked fiercely, but though they had come very near us they had not been able to break through. During the day the enemy had remained quiet, contenting themselves with sniping, and now evidently, under cover of darkness, they had withdrawn to another position.

"Well, I suppose we shall push on now," I said to Goyle.

"Yes, I expect so," he answered.

Our orders to advance came at four o'clock. Goyle came down to give the necessary instructions to platoon commanders. We were to push forward straight to our front, keeping under cover as much as possible. He said he believed that the ground was all clear in front of us, but that it would be as well to take precautions.

Evans and I therefore led our platoons down a ditch which led direct to the front. We eventually came out by a large farm building which a day or two ago had been in the hands of the Germans. It had been known to the British troops as "the hospital," because the Germans had hoisted a Red Cross flag on a pole on the roof. But "the hospital" had also been used by the enemy as an observing station, and our guns had been obliged to shell it on two or three occasions. We examined the building with interest. The place was evidently a dairy farm on a large scale, for three sides were cowsheds, and there was a big store of hay. At the far end was the dwelling-house, over which the Red Cross had been hoisted. The place had perhaps been used as a hospital, for in the bottom room we found a long riding boot, which had been cut off a wounded man, and a blood-soaked pair of the well-known blue-grey breeches. However, on going up on to the roof we found the facilities for seeing over our lines so remarkable that the shells from our guns were evidently justly placed.

I made the tour of the farm with the doctor of the Dorchesters, who was thinking of taking it over at a hospital himself. When we came down from the roof we found two farm girls outside. They asked us anxiously if it would be safe for them to stay there that night, and we assured them it would. They said they had gone off a mile or two for two or three days, but now they had come back to look after the cows. They were a pair of very cool young ladies, who seemed to regard the German occupation of their farm as no more than a heavy rainstorm, to be avoided while it lasted, but not to be worried about once it was over. The doctor and I went round to look at the cowsheds. The beasts were all in their stalls, some evidently suffering a good deal from want of milking.

In the first shed we came to there was a most appalling stench. The doctor sniffed and said he thought it was something dead. We examined the cows that were lying down, but they were all alive. Then the doctor made an orderly rake over all the straw. He said that the Germans had a habit of hiding dead men under straw, if they were vacating a place, just by way of providing a pleasant surprise for any tired British soldiers who might make the straw their bed. However, there were no corpses in the cowshed, and we never discovered the cause of the smell, though it was strong and nasty enough to prevent my ever forgetting it.

On coming out of the farm I found the Dorchester Regiment passing by. After lying about in a trench, hardly seeing more than the men in one's own platoon, it was quite a change to see another regiment and have a talk to the officers about their experiences in the past few days. It was interesting to hear how the next-door regiment had fared in the night attack, and if they had met much opposition in gaining the village they had been told to take. One subaltern, with a scrubby ten days' growth of beard on his chin, grinned as though he thought he knew me as he went by, and said: "Who'd have thought we were being brought up to do this?"

I looked at him, and suddenly recognised a fellow who had been a cadet with me at Sandhurst. It did, indeed, seem droll to look back on the days when we had drilled in the same squad together and studied tactics in the same class, without ever, I am afraid, any serious thoughts of war. Well, anyway, now our learning was being put to the test, and as I watched the boy now become a man march by with his company, all muddy in the trenches, with his few worldly possessions slung from his belt, I thought that he, at any rate, was a good advertisement for Sandhurst.

"Where are you going—do you know?" I called.

He shrugged his shoulders and pointed away across the fields. It was growing dusk, and I began to wonder where we were going. We had been halted by the farm some time now. I turned back to my platoon, who were lying on some straw against a wall. I thought I would go and find some of the other platoon commanders and hear if there was any news. But this plan was frustrated, Evans and the others were nowhere to be found. I asked my sergeant if he knew where the rest of the company was. He said he did not. It was my business, of course, not his, to know, and he—wretched man—having been asleep, knew this perfectly well.

After a search round the farm I came to the conclusion that the company had gone off somewhere and that I was left. Here was a pretty kettle of fish. Goyle would not thank me for losing a whole platoon. The company must be found again at once. The difficulty was they might have gone off in any direction. I questioned the men. Some thought they had seen the captain going back the way we had come; others had seen nothing. To go back the way we had come would probably be putting oneself too far back if wanted. I eventually decided to cut straight across a field and reach a road which would take me to the same village as the Dorchesters were going to. In this way I should have them between myself and the enemy, and so eliminate the risk of being cut off, and also should be moving along towards the enemy in the same direction as presumably my company was moving.

It was by now quite dark, and, crossing the field, we nearly fell into an empty trench which the Germans had held. The most noticeable thing about the trench was the murderous field of fire it afforded. The trench had evidently been sighted by a past master in the art of war. On reaching the road I decided to stay there for a while until some one came along from whom I could ask questions. It was rather jumpy work to be isolated by oneself with a platoon without quite knowing where one was. To my great relief, after a few minutes a company from my regiment came along, followed by Goyle at the head of my own company, and I was able to join up.

It appeared that in the interval since we had parted the company had been ordered to entrench themselves in three different places, and then moved on again, and so, as Goyle did not seem to mind once I had joined up again safely, I was very glad I had missed all the unnecessary excitement. It was characteristic of Goyle that he never found fault with anything his subalterns did unless it led to trouble. As I had got there alright somehow, and not been wanted in the meantime, he did not blame me for getting lost.

We marched along for a little way down the road, and then swung to the right down another road, which led through a straggling village. The cottages were all in darkness, but they looked very inviting, and I think each man wished heartily that he was going to sleep in one instead of marching on into the night.

After passing through the village we came out on to a straight road flanked by two deep ditches. After going a few hundred yards along this road we were told to halt, climb over the ditch, and entrench. This we did.

When all was snug and compact for the night Goyle and I went back to the village to let the Dorchesters know what we had done. We found several of the officers in the kitchen of a small wine shop. They had got a fire going, and were making coffee, and this, with a bottle of rum found in the cellar, and the remains of the day's rations, promised an excellent supper. I had some bread and cheese left in my haversack, and shared this with Goyle; we were given a mug of coffee each, and joined the others at the table. After the excitements of the evening the coffee and rum were welcome.

As we were having supper I heard some groans, and suddenly noticed a huge Uhlan lying flat on his back in the corner. He was breathing with difficulty, and every now and then seemed to be trying to wriggle along the floor. One of the Dorchester officers told me that the man had been found in a ditch and brought in by our men. He was shot straight through the stomach. They had sent up for the doctor, but the latter was unable to come down that night. Supper proceeded smoothly, uninterrupted by the groans of the Uhlan, who was only half-conscious, but at times evidently in great pain.

"I say," said one of the Dorchesters' officers, "I propose sleeping here. I don't much fancy having that fellow in the room all night."

It was then decided to move the Uhlan to an empty house opposite, where he died by himself, and was found on his knees, with his head contorted between them in a last effort to rise, in the morning.

14

In Front of La Bassée

At daybreak the order came to advance. A and C Companies were to form the firing-line, B and D Companies were to be in support. We formed the right of the brigade, and had to get in touch with the Westshires, who were on the left of the —th Brigade, on our right. The initiative of the attack rested with A and C Companies; our task was to follow behind over the ground they had gained and be ready to come up into line with them should they lose many men or find themselves hard pressed. The enemy we knew to be holding a group of houses about 700 yards away. The ground sloped gently back from these houses to the outskirts of the town. My company, B Company, under Goyle, had been extended during the night, in a field to the right of the road, and had thrown up a low earthwork parapet. We now lay behind this while A and C Companies pushed through us to the front.

The parapet proved none too high, for as soon as the men in front showed themselves a brisk fire came from the enemy in the houses. We all lay flat on the ground, and the bullets came *phzz-phzz* over us, missing us, as it seemed, by an inch or two. There is an old military adage that the man who thinks each bullet he hears if going to hit him is making active service a torture to himself. Now, it is all very well to preach the value of being philosophical in warfare and to recommend the man under fire not to think about being hit, but that peculiar sharp little whistle which a bullet makes as it passes one's ear takes a good deal of getting used to, and one's first instinct as one hears it is to slide as deep and far into the ground as possible. We all lay there with our noses flat in the earth, wondering how the fellows in front were getting on and when it would be our turn to get up.

The opportunity came pretty soon, for, as the company in front seemed to be held up by the enemy in the houses, Goyle decided to send round a flanking party, and sent off No. 7 and 8 platoons to work their way round on the right. This plan proved successful, and A Company was able to get ahead. Goyle now signalled for the two platoons, which had remained with him, to advance. We rose and moved forward in extended order for 300 yards and then lay down again.

After a few minutes Goyle exclaimed: "Hullo!—our fellows have reached the houses." Looking through my glasses, I saw some of our men in the gardens of the houses, and as there was no fighting going on the Germans had evidently withdrawn. Goyle decided that we would push on, and told Evans and me to join up by the houses with two platoons which had gone round by the flank. We were to search the houses thoroughly, and take up a line on the other side of them. On our way forward we came on the results of some work we had heard going on during the night. Just before we reached the houses we found three men from the Westshires in a ditch. One was dead, the others too badly hit to crawl. It appears they had been sent out on patrol the night before, and, coming on the German lines, had got shot down. As I had been out on patrol myself on the other side of the road the same night, I reflected that my patrol had been lucky to escape the same fate.

The two wounded men had been lying there for some time, and were very glad to be found. The worst side of patrol work is the risk of not being found or it not being possible to bring wounded men in. We sent the two wounded men back to the ambulance, and asked for a party to be sent up to bury the other. I took the dead man's rifle myself. It was very bloody and nasty, but I felt it would be a good companion, as apart from a rifle and bayonet being twice as useful as a revolver and sword (no one carries the latter), a rifle is also a very good disguise for an officer. If he is holding his rifle, as the men always do, at the trail in an advance, he is indistinguishable to the enemy.

Especially was this the case at one time, when the enemy had got used to looking out for a gentleman with a revolver in one hand, a walking-stick in the other, and a pair of field-glasses slung round his neck, advancing slightly ahead of the line of men, and waving instructions to them with the stick. Nowadays the wise officer keeps well in a line with his men, and gives as few indications by hand signals to halt or advance etc., as possible.

I got most of the blood off the rifle with some grass, and, armed with it and the bayonet, I felt much more secure as we made our way through the houses. The Germans had evidently spent a day or two round the houses, for just behind we found a straw-lined ditch, which they had slept in and partially converted to a trench. We lined this ditch, which gave good cover against stray bullets, and waited for further orders. While we were waiting, Edwards, who had charge of the flanking party, pushed out to the right to get in touch with the Westshires, and Evans and I went back to have a look at the houses and see if the enemy had left any souvenirs behind.

One of the buildings was the village wine shop, and a party of German officers had evidently used it as their headquarters for the night. They appeared to have had a rare time in the place. Half-emptied glasses of wine had been left on the bar counter and on the table; bottles and glasses lay smashed on the floor; every bottle from the shelves behind the bar had been taken down and either drunk or broken and the contents spilt over the floor. Two chairs lay broken, and all the pictures were smashed, presumably by cockshies with bottles and glasses. From the look of things the officers must have all been extremely drunk.

While we were in the wine shop the order came for us to close up on A Company, who had pushed some distance forward. The ground at this point sloped up to some more cottages and farm buildings which lay at the top of the rise. A and C Companies had worked their way through the cottages and lined out beyond them facing the outskirts of the town. They were unable to go any farther, as the ground in front was a dead flat stretch of root crops, which the Germans could sweep with rifle and machine-gun fire. The cottages in front to a certain extent covered the advance up to this point, but not completely, as Mulligan, in charge of the right platoon of the next supporting company discovered to his cost.

We were advancing in extended order up the rise, my company being well protected by the cottages, but Mulligan had a gap in the buildings in front of him. About halfway across the field he evidently came into range of a German machine-gun. The gun opened a brisk fire and in as many seconds twenty of his men were down, Mulligan himself getting a bullet through the shoulder, and his servant, who was beside him, being killed. From an infantryman's point of view a Maxim is like water to a mad dog. It will stop him when nothing else will.

There is something particularly deterring about the sound of a Maxim, with its *ping-ping-ping-ping* as it sweeps down a line of advancing troops, spurting lead like a hosepipe. The great art from an infantryman's point of view is to locate these guns, and avoid going over ground they cover. It is, humanly speaking, hopeless to try to advance straight against them. Word soon goes along a line, "They've got a Maxim along that road," or "Machine-guns are on that corner of the field or gap in the hedge," and the road, or corner of the field, or gap in the hedge is avoided like a plague spot accordingly.

After we had lain behind the cottages on the rise for a little while, the commander of A Company sent back to say he would like a platoon from the supports sent up to him. Goyle told me to take up No. 6. Hutson, who was commanding A Company, was a capital fellow to work under, and was moving about behind his trenches giving directions to the men as coolly as if he had been on manoeuvres instead of only separated by a root field from the first line of the German Army. He showed me the bit of trench he wanted my platoon to occupy, gave some instructions about putting out an advanced post, and said the officers of A Company wore having a stew cooked in the kitchen of one of the cottages, if I would care to come in when it was dark and all was straight for the night. He said he did not think we should try to advance any farther that night, but hold on where we were.

I lined my men out along the section of trench I was to occupy, which had mostly still to be made, and got them to work. It was growing dusk, and buildings along the outskirts of the town were standing out clearly against the sky-line. Just in front of us was what appeared to be a large factory. As I watched I saw a shell crash against the roof of the factory, followed by another and another. Soon flames sprang from a corner of the building, but still the shells were sent against it, and in ten minutes the whole building was ablaze.

Our guns stopped firing when the smoke and fire showed they had done their work. Dark figures could be seen running about from point to point silhouetted against the flames. Our men fired at the figures, and made jokes about the discomfiture of the enemy, who could not move now without being shown up by the flames, while they themselves were secure in the darkness.

Then as I watched I saw a very dashing piece of work on the part of the enemy, for up galloped a section of horse artillery right into the firing-line, unlimbered, and opened fire. Their target was soon plain: a row of haystacks just behind our lines. In five minutes these stacks, too, were blazing merrily, and our lines were lit up as clearly as the Germans'.

The whole scene made a wonderful stage battle effect, with the two rival lines of trenches and the flames behind each shooting luridly to the sky.

Later Hutson came up to me.

"By Jove!" he said, "my young subaltern did a good bit of work just now. You know when those German guns started on our stacks. Well, he got three men with buckets, filled 'em at a pump, and dashed at the first stack and tried to put it out. A bit of a fireman, to get to work like that while the object he was trying to extinguish was still under shell fire."

I am glad to say that the deed of the young subaltern referred to was mentioned in dispatches and that he received the D.S.O. and the three men with him the D.C.M.

15

A Night Patrol

The regiment was acting as advance guard to the brigade, so considerable responsibility rested on Goyle, who was senior officer of the three companies employed. Goyle had been through the war from the beginning, and had learnt the difference between reckless dash and careful handling of men. Goyle had had four of his subalterns killed and most of his original company replaced by reinforcements. He had held the canal bank at Mons and fought slowly backwards from house to house at Le Cateau. What he did not know of the Germans and their methods of fighting no general knew, nor staff officer with red-banded, brass-rimmed cap. Perhaps the generals and their staff officers knew as much theoretically and had learnt a good deal from the result of actions in which the divisions and units under their command had been engaged, but none knew more than Goyle, who was a plain regimental officer and lived daily in the firing-line. Had many but he been in command that night the advance guard would have been cut up.

We had covered the first part of our march uneventfully, and were now moving along a stretch of open road which ran between two deep ditches with plough-land on either side. The Dorchesters were following us, and they, we knew, had reached a village about half a mile behind. Goyle was from the first extremely anxious not to let the gap between ourselves and the Dorchesters get too wide. Our orders were to halt on a cross-road at some point farther down along the road on which we were marching. It was quite dark, and we were proceeding very slowly, as we were uncertain of the whereabouts or strength of the enemy.

Goyle had got all the men off the road, and was making them move single file by companies along the ditches. We proceeded some distance in this way, but no crossroads could be found, and after a bit

199

Goyle halted and sent back for further instructions. He discovered at the same time that communication had not been maintained with the brigade on the right, and that the Dorchesters showed no inclination to leave the village they had reached, but were disposed to billet there. In fact, everything pointed to a slight muddle having arisen, as a result of which the three companies of my regiment might be severe sufferers in their isolated position if the enemy suddenly attacked.

It was the sort of occasion when many officers less experienced than Goyle might have done something which would have led to a disaster. Many, for instance, would have pushed boldly on until they found the cross-roads or met the enemy. They would have said that those were their orders and that it was not for them to wonder whether there was any mistake. However, Goyle was not of this sort. He believed in using his own judgment and acting as circumstances seemed to dictate. His first concern was for the lives of his men, which he would throw away as lightly as his own if necessary, but which he always guarded jealously against the possible perils of tactical mistakes.

"I don't like this," he said once or twice, as we were standing there waiting for the reply to the message he had sent back. "It is all very well, you know, but if they came for us now in any strength we should get scuppered."

It was dark, and we seemed a long way out along the road from the other troops. I understood what he meant, and saw the danger. Presently the orderly returned with a written message from the commanding officer: "You are to go on as far as the R in ——, and remain in the village for the night."

Goyle pulled out his map, and we bent over it. —— was a village of a few cottages, apparently about a quarter of a mile down the road. I could see Goyle did not like the order. "It is all very well," he said; "probably the enemy are in the village—a nice trap we shall be walking into. I shall send on a patrol, and if the village is held I shan't move on till daylight, when we have got some reinforcements up."

It was then decided that I should take out a patrol and go and scout the village. "Take a lance-corporal and a man with you," said Goyle; "and when you get to the village one of you go into the first house, leaving the other two outside; if the one who goes into the house does not come out, another is to follow him in, and if he stays too, the third is to come back and tell me. If we hear shots and none of you return we shall know the village is occupied."

"Very good, sir," I said; and, wishing I was anywhere else, I went off to get the patrol. I called my platoon together, explained the work on hand, and asked for volunteers. I got a N.C.O. without difficulty, but there was no response when I asked for a man. Much disgusted at the want of spirit in the men, I was preparing to go off alone with the lance-corporal rather than force anyone to go with me, when a man stepped out of the ranks and made the party complete.

Afterwards Jenkins, my soldier servant, from whom I used to get tips about handling the men and various bits of barrack-room gossip, explained to me why I had got an N.C.O. easily enough, but had had difficulty in getting a man. It appeared that the men had a rooted dislike to patrols composed of an officer, a non-commissioned officer, and a man, as they considered the man was always made the victim of the enterprise, being sent on when the danger point was reached to draw fire. He said that had I asked for two men they would have come forward willingly, but, having got the N.C.O., no one cared to offer himself to take the place of the private.

I saw what Jenkins meant, and decided to remember the point for future guidance. As a matter of fact, I had decided that we should all go together, anyway until the occasion came for entering the houses, when it would be time enough to arrange who should go first.

Having got my N.C.O. and man together, I explained to them the work that was on foot, and said that at the first shot from the enemy each was to run for himself, and that no one was to wait to reply to the fire; all we had to do was to find out whether or not the place was occupied. Liking the job less each minute, we started off down the road. After going a little way it occurred to me that an old military rule was to keep a Maxim on a road at night, and that we should get rather in the way of this if the enemy had one and opened fire. Accordingly I ordered the patrol off the road on to the plough-land beside. This was a good manoeuvre, as we were able to creep over the soft soil noiselessly. We felt our way on for some distance, until I saw two dark objects. These were the first of the houses we had to explore.

Praying fervently that they might be empty, I led the way towards them. Suddenly there was a sharp burst of fire ahead along a front of about fifty yards. The shots could not have been fired from more than ten yards range. We had evidently all but walked into a German trench. The enemy had heard us, and blazed into the night. The effect of the shots suddenly fired out of nothing was most startling. As one man we all three turned and bolted in the opposite direction. The corporal dropped his rifle, I lost my cap; the private, being a fine sprinter, got slightly ahead, and we all three ran like mad. After a couple of hundred yards I went head over heels into a ditch. The corporal paused a moment to see if I had been hit, but continued as soon as I got up; the man kept an unchecked course for home, looking neither to the right nor the left.

In the fall I slightly dislocated my knee, but this was as nothing, and, hardly hindered by a limp, I followed at full speed in the wake of the rout, the man now holding a good lead, the corporal lying second, and myself a bad third. I bethought me as I ran that we should probably draw the fire of our own men, who would think we were the enemy, and halloaed: "Goyle—Goyle—this is the patrol returning."

"Shut up, you blithering idiot," I heard his voice from the road; "do you want all Germany to know where we are?"

I flung myself on the ground beside him and breathlessly reported what had happened. "H'm," said Goyle, "just what I thought. I shan't try to occupy that village tonight."

Just then the major commanding the regiment and adjutant, who had been back with the reserve company, came up. "Well, what is it, Goyle?" said the major testily; "why don't you push on into the village?"

The major was a very gallant officer, with considerable war experience behind him. To his mind "dash" was the great thing. But the major's experiences had been chiefly in savage warfare, and he had no knowledge of German methods. He had only come out from England two days before to take the place of our colonel, who had been wounded.

Goyle pointed to me, said that he had sent out a patrol, and that the village was occupied. "Oh," said the adjutant, "probably only two or three half-scared Uhlans. You ought to have tackled them and brought back their helmets—this to me.

I offered with acid politeness to indicate the position of the "Uhlans" so that the adjutant could go out himself and get their helmets.

"I think the enemy are entrenched, sir," said Goyle to the major.

"Well, have at them and drive them out," the latter answered.

"We are rather isolated here, sir, and we are too weak to attack the village by ourselves."

"Maybe—maybe—I should push on, though," the major answered.

"If you will excuse me, sir, I feel the responsibility rather too great—if you would take command of the attack, sir." This was a master-stroke on Goyle's part, as it brought home to the major the responsibility of throwing his men without proper support against a position of unknown strength in the dark. He hummed and hawed, and finally decided to leave things as they were till daylight, and returned with the adjutant to the reserve company.

As things turned out, it was lucky for all of us that Goyle had been firm about advancing farther; for, so far from there only being a few half-scared Uhlans ahead of us, we discovered afterwards that the Germans were in force and strongly entrenched, and any attempt at attack by the three companies must have failed disastrously.

When the major had gone Goyle decided to move back, so as to get in closer touch with the Dorchesters. We withdrew, therefore, to the outskirts of the village, lined out on the plough-land on either side of the road, and set the men to entrench.

16

With the Supports

The Support trenches lay along a road about fifty yards behind the firing-line. The trenches themselves were made partly from a ditch by the side of the road, and partly excavated from a ploughed field which ran out in the direction of the enemy. The firing-line trenches were beyond in the ploughed field itself; beyond the plough-land again came a stretch of root crop, and at the end of this the enemy.

The Westshires were holding the firing-line, and we were close up behind them in support! In spite of the narrow margin between the supports and firing-line life was a good deal easier for the supports. Indeed, we felt ourselves onlookers compared to the Westshires in front. The ground sloped gently down from their trenches to the road. They could not move without showing up against the sky-line, while we, by crouching, could move about our trenches with comparative freedom.

But the chief blessing of being in support lay in the fact that we were not directly responsible for giving the first alarm. The onus of waiting and watching for the German attack lay on the Westshires, and our men felt themselves to be more or less onlookers for the day, and lay about reading the newspapers and smoking. Evans and I found plenty to occupy ourselves during the afternoon. There was a small farm just by the side of our trench, protected from view by a row of cottages. The owners of the farm had gone the day before, when there had been an attack on the village, and left their home just as it was. We took over the farm for our own use, got a fire going in the kitchen, and set our servants to work to prepare dinner.

Jenkins, my servant, had been a chauffeur valet before the war, and had great ideas how things ought to be done. These ideas had on oc-casion been reduced to making tea during a halt by the roadside in a small black and dirty pot, which he kept fastened to his pack, but with a kitchen stove to cook over and an unlimited supply of crockery he was in his element.

Having annexed the farm as an officers' mess and installed Jenkins in the kitchen we made a tour of the yard. Here we found several things which wanted doing. First there was the farm dog, who had been left behind chained to his kennel. The dog had had nothing to eat for two days, and was ravenous. We got him a large bone and loosed him, so that if we had to scurry he would not have to stay behind. Then we found some cows in a shed in great pain from want of milking. There was a man in my platoon who had been a dairyman, and I set him to work on them. In a barn we found a quantity of straw, which we sent down to the trenches. Finally we got soap and towels from a bedroom, and repaired to the pump for a much-needed cleaning.

After washing ourselves we went out for a stroll before dinner. We found a little group standing in the lee of the cottage across the road— the adjutant of the Westshires, the regimental doctor, two stretcher-bearers, and an N.C.O. A man had been hit in the trench just ahead of us, and the doctor had been sent for to come up from the field-ambulance. The doctor had just sent word up to the trench to find out the nature of the man's injuries. If he was severely wounded and required immediate attention, the doctor was prepared to send up his stretcher-bearers to have him brought down, but it would be a difficult job and exposing men's lives, and the doctor wanted, if possible, to leave the man there till dark.

Doctors attached to regiments have many difficult points to settle, and occasions like this often arise when it is hard for them to decide whether to risk more lives to save one. They are called upon sometimes to go up and attend to cases in all sorts of impossible places, and in the firing-line the old cry of "Send for the doctor" is not quite so easily answered as in other places.

We left the group by the cottage waiting for the reply about the nature of the wounded man's injuries. Not a head showed from the trench where he was lying. The trench itself, though only twenty yards or so away, was hardly visible in the field. Glad it was not our turn to lie like logs in it all the day, we went on down the village street. Nearly all the cottages were empty, but in one we came on a group of inhabitants who had remained. They had all collected in a kitchen and were having a last meal round their table. They had got a little bread and some coffee, which they were sharing with three private soldiers, who in exchange had contributed a tin of bully beef.

It made a strange sight to see the weeping, frightened women and the tired dusty soldiers who had come to defend them. The women had given the men a place round the fire, and were waiting on them attentively. The privates could speak no French and the peasants no English, so conversation was impossible, but an interchange of thought could be read in the eyes of both parties; the women looking on the men sadly and devoutedly, realising they had come there perhaps to give their lives for them, and across the men's faces would come a look of appreciation for the hot comforting coffee, and at other times a look of inscrutable purposefulness, which is hard to describe, but which all our men wear in France, and which is symbolic of the spirit which is carrying them through the campaign.

Seeing officers outside, one of the women came out. I said "good-morning" to her in French, and with a delighted "*Ah, Monsieur, vous parlez Français*" she addressed herself to me excitedly. It appeared that her husband had been missing since the day before. She was very anxious about him. Two officers had come to the cottage, asked him some questions, and then taken him away with them. She had not seen the man since. What did I think could have become of him? I asked her some questions about the officers who had taken her husband away, and from her description gathered that they were a captain and subaltern in the British Army. As the Westshire Regiment was the only regiment that I knew had been in the village since the Germans left it, I felt sure the officers the woman referred to must be from that regiment.

Accordingly I went back to ask the adjutant of the Westshires if he could give any information on the subject. He told me that when the regiment had got up to the village the day before they had searched the cottages and found a man in one of the upper rooms behaving suspiciously with a lamp by a window which looked on the German lines. They had taken the man off with them and sent him back to the rear, where he would probably be tried for his life for a spy. This put me in an awkward position, as I did not know what to tell the poor woman, who, whatever her husband had done, was herself innocent of any evil intentions. I contended myself with telling her that her husband was in British hands, and that she might rest assured he would be fairly treated.

Another difficulty then presented itself. The little party of women in the cottage all wished to leave the village. They had collected their few most cherished possessions together in a cart and proposed to go off as soon as it was dark. But this could not be permitted, as the noise of the cart, which would have to go along a road that ran through our lines, would have attracted the enemy's attention and drawn their fire on our men. The women refused to leave the cart with their treasures behind and the situation seemed to have reached an *impasse*. Finally, after interviewing the colonel of the Westshires, I was able to get permission for them to take their cart, provided they kept it along the grassy side of the road.

I shall never forget the little procession as it moved off after dark. First the cart, drawn by an old horse with a woman leading it followed by a sorrowful little procession of women and children with quick, frightened steps and bowed heads. They were leaving their village, their homes, nearly all their belongings, and the little plots of garden and weaving looms which were their livelihood, to go out to the country beyond—which had always appeared in the little hemisphere of their lives as a strange land dealing hardly with wandering strangers. They were going away and would, perhaps, never see their village again. (Alas, indeed, they never did.) Well may they have wondered what they had done to bring such misery about their heads—misery embodied in the Scriptural curse of old: War, rape, desolation, and famine.

However, there is little sentiment in war, and as we watched them go we had not more than a passing thought for them. We were chiefly conscious of having a farm to ourselves, and the prospect of a night of unusual comfort for the firing-line.

Jenkins had made great preparations while we were away, and had a two-course dinner ready for us—roast chickens and stewed apples. We fell to on this heartily, and then sat round the kitchen stove drinking hot rum and water. We turned in early, two of us using two beds and the other two mattresses on the floor. With the Westshires in front of us we were carefree for the night. An hour before dawn we were called, and went back to the trenches to rouse the men to stand to arms. Then we went to bed again and slept till eight.

We pulled the kitchen table out to the garden for breakfast, and made a capital meal of fried eggs and bread and marmalade. We sat over breakfast smoking cigarettes and drinking last cups of tea It seemed odd to be living such a leisurely life 700 yards from the enemy, but the cottages in front secured us as long they did not use artillery. However, this was to come later. An artillery observing officer came to fix up a field telephone just by our breakfast table. He expressed his opinion that the enemy had got their guns up, and that the day would be lively.

"Well," said Goyle, "perhaps we had better get back to the trench for a bit anyway." Our trench was only ten yards off, just the other side of the garden, and we stepped into it. Scarcely had we done so than—*crash!*—a Black Maria fell fair and square on the farm where we had been sleeping. It was a matter of seconds, and what happened to the artillery observing officer, whom we had left behind adjusting his telephone, I do not know. Perhaps he lived. Artillery observing officers have a knack of living in places where any other man would be killed. However, we had no time to speculate on his fate, for a minute later another high-explosive shell burst fifty yards over the trench, followed by a second twenty-five yards over us. The enemy were shortening their range. The men stirred uneasily in their dugouts. No rat in a trap could feel worse than an infantryman in a trench when a big gun is searching for him with high explosive. *BANG!* A shell burst on the other side of the road—ten yards from us. The next would undoubtedly do it.

"Here," I called to Goyle, "what about this? They are getting our range."

"We had better quit," he said. "Don't let the men run—file out slowly to the right, and lie down behind that bank there. The other platoon must stay; they are not being molested at present."

With as much dignity as possible, considering I expected a Black Maria in the back at any moment, I led the men out of the trench, and we threaded our way gingerly back to the bank indicated, from which we watched the vicious demolition of our empty trench.

17

Between Actions

Just before dusk I was sent up with my platoon to join D Company, who had more line than the number of men in the company could safely hold. After being shown the section of ground where my men were wanted, I went off to join the other officers of the company, who were having a bit of dinner in a cottage, leaving the men to improve the trench, and telling Jenkins, my soldier-servant, to make a good big dugout for us both.

It is interesting now to record that the officer commanding the company to which I was lent was a man I had known in times of peace and loathed to the point which drives a man to homicide. He was a fine great fellow, but a bit rough with subalterns, and had, as he no doubt thought for my own good, made my life a burden to me when I joined the regiment. I often used to say to myself, when discipline and mess etiquette prevented my replying to his remarks to me in the ante-room in days of peace: "My sainted aunt, if ever I get alone with you in the desert, my friend, I'll shoot."

For two or three years we never spoke to each other, and then suddenly I found myself sent up to serve under him in the firing-line in front of La Bassée. How circumstances alter cases. He had me in his hands then. Had he been the bully I thought him, there were a hundred dirty jobs he could have made me do. He could have sent me out on patrol or with messages to the next regiment. There were many nasty thing, which had to be done that night. But all he said, when I came up and reported myself as having been sent up to reinforce him with a platoon, was: "Hullo, old chap. Look here, I just want you to put your men along here do you see?" indicating the gap he wanted filled "and when you've done that, come into the cottage and have a bit of dinner."

It was hospitable at a time when each man earned his own rations for the day, and I had none left. The putting out of patrols and walking up and down the line he did himself rather than ask me, whose job it was as his subaltern for the time being. A few days later, when I was hit, he was one of the first people to come up to me, and he was himself killed five minutes later, gallantly leading a charge to drive the Germans back from the spot where the wounded were dying.

While we were having dinner, the other subalterns and myself compared notes about the different quarters we had for the night; one saying he had not room to lie down in his dugout; another that he had found a lot of hay and made a fine lair; and the machinegun officer saying that he was best off of all, as he had his guns peeping from the window of a bedroom above, and proposed to spend the night in bed by the side of them..

When the meal was over and we had had a smoke, we dispersed to the different sections of the defence we were holding. I found that Jenkins had made a beautiful dugout, lined it with straw, and roofed it with some V-shaped pieces of thatch which the peasants in that part of France use to protect their fruit. He had allowed just the right space for me to lie down, and done everything he could think of that would enable us to spend the night comfortably. Jenkins in private life was a chauffeur-valet, of a fastidious, easily ruffled, and slightly grasping disposition. However, though he would have died rather than wear some of my old clothes, he was so well able to adapt himself to the war that he won the D.C.M.

Having looked along the trench and moved the group sentry to a point just near the dugout, I settled down beside Jenkins on the straw. Jenkins and I shared a little rum I had left over in my flask from the day's rations, and, feeling very warm and good inside, closed our eyes. My guardian angel was with me that evening, for I could not sleep, and Jenkins, who could, kept grunting, which got on my nerves so near my ear, so I decided to take some of the straw and lie down behind the trench outside.

It was very dark, and the outline of the group sentry could just be seen against the parapet. From where I had been in the dugout I could not see either of the sentries. As we were in the front line, with nothing but a stretch of plough-land between ourselves and the Germans and all the men in the trench were asleep, those two sentries were pretty important. I lay there watching them with half-closed eyes. One was resting with his head on the parapet (which is permissible as long as the other keeps a sharp watch), but to my horror I saw the other, after about ten minutes, turn round, sit against the parapet with his back to the enemy, and deliberately drop his head on his arms and go to sleep.

We now had no one keeping watch over us at all, and there was nothing to stop the Germans creeping over and bayoneting a trench full of sleeping men. My first instinct was to march the sentry straight off under arrest, then I remembered the penalty, and that he was only a boy, and that it was many days and nights since the men had had proper sleep. So I crept towards him, gave him a crack under the jaw with my fist, which would effectively keep him awake for the rest of his turn of duty, said, "You dare to turn round with your back to the enemy," and lay down again. I remember waking up uneasily every quarter of an hour through the night and looking to see if the sentry was keeping awake, and being reassured by a plaintive snuffling as the boy looked ahead and rubbed his chin.

At 4 a.m. a regiment came to take over our lines, and we were sent back in reserve. We marched back about a mile to a big empty farm, where we were told we were going to spend the day. I had rejoined my own company, and, as caterer for the company officers' mess, set about getting breakfast for the five officers.

One of the latter, Edwards, was fresh out to the Front, and had not quite got out of the way of being waited on by mess waiters. We had sat down to the meal, which I had got ready on a table in the garden. Edwards came up late, and found there was no tea left, so I sent him to the kitchen to get some. Later we all wanted another cup, and I dispatched him again, as he was the junior of the party, and I did not see why I should do all the work. He came back and said there was no one there; what was he to do about the tea? I said, "Make it." He said he did not know how to. I took him gently by the arm and led him to the kitchen to show him.

When we had finished breakfast, Goyle and the senior platoon commanders lit their pipes, while I cleared away the things. Edwards pulled out his pipe too. But I said, "No, my boy; you help here." I had an armful of crockery as I spoke, which I was taking to wash up. Looking rather hurt, he followed me into the kitchen, carrying a teaspoon.

"I don't see why I should do all this," he said, as we were washing up.

"Don't you, my boy?" I said, sharply. "And do you see any reason for me doing it?" He did not answer. "It may not be one of the things you learnt at Sandhurst," I continued, "but when you've been engaged in this campaign a little longer, you'll discover that if you don't bally well shift for yourself you'll starve."

He was a good boy all the same, and got a bullet through the knee leading his men at ——, and is a guest of the *Kaiser* now.

For lunch we had a Mc'Conochie. Mc'Ccnochie is a form of tinned stew, and very succulent if properly cooked, as vegetables and a rich gravy are contained in the tin. The usual way is to put the tin in a saucepan of boiling water, let it boil for a while, and then take it out and open it. However, that day as we were in a hurry—we had had orders to take over the Westshires' trenches at midnight—I put the tin straight on the fire, thinking to warm it up quicker. We were sitting round talking when Evans suddenly exclaimed, "Gad, look at that tin!"

We looked and saw it swelling itself out. The gravy had turned to steam, and the thing was on the point of bursting. I seized the tongs and snatched it from the fire, placing it on the table. The thing still seemed to be swelling gently.

"Quick," said Goyle, "prick it—it will go off."

I opened my clasp knife and gave it a jab. There was a sound like an engine-whistle, and a jet of gravy steam shot into Goyle's eye.

"Oh, oh, you blithering idiot," he shouted, dancing about the room with his hand clapped to his eye.

I watched the tin, wondering if all the stew had turned to steam. However, happily it had not, and we had a good meal.

Alter lunch I strolled across to have a look at the field-dressing station, which was in one of the farm outbuildings.

The doctor was attending to one or two wounded who came in, but not having a very busy time. I watched him at work for a little while. He was wonderfully thorough considering that his ward consisted of an open yard and his material a box of dressings, a pair of scissors, and a bottle of iodine. He stripped off the field bandages of each man that came in and put on fresh dressings. One fellow walked in with a bullet straight through his chest. He was deathly pale, but he stood up while they took off his jacket and cut his shirt away, and looked down quite unconcerned at the blood pouring from the hole through him.

At four o'clock we were told we were wanted in the firing-line again. Goyle made the men take off their greatcoats and advised the officers to put away their mackintoshes.

This last piece of advice was very sound. An officer wearing a mackintosh is a conspicuous target in a line of men, and many have met their death through doing it. Officers will carry rifles, cover their field-glasses with khaki cloth, wear web equipment, and take all sorts of precautions to make themselves as like the men as possible, and then the first time a shower of rain comes put on their mackintoshes and forget to take them off again when they advance. They might just as well wear surplices.

18

"The —th Brigade Will Attack ——"

We thought we should have to attack that day, as we knew the powers that be were most anxious for —— to be taken.

The regiment had been, so to speak, in the forefront of the battle for the past two or three days; that is to say, we had not had any troops between ourselves and the enemy, and, though the fighting had never been of a brisk nature, nevertheless the men were feeling the strain of constant watchfulness and going without sleep. Even if there is not much firing it is not a restful feeling to have nothing but a stretch of open plough-land between oneself and the enemy, and to feel one may be called upon to advance over the plough-land at any minute. It was a nasty stretch of open country, swept and raked from every corner by the enemy's machine-guns, and to lie there waiting for the order to get up and cross it was rather like sitting inspecting a stiff fence.

Greatly to our relief the Westshire Regiment had been sent up to relieve us at 4 a.m. and we had gone back in support. We had handed over the trenches to them without much reluctance, and with an easy prescience that we had had our share of work, and that it was the turn for a regiment fresh from reserve to come up and take our place.

After being relieved we were marched back to a sugar refinery a mile behind, and here we fully expected to spend the day. The men were issued out rations, and the officers made preparations for breakfast. There was a nice house belonging to the manager of the sugar refinery, and in a kitchen we found some crockery and a fire, also the caretaker of the manager's house and his wife. The latter made us a pot of tea, and with our morning issue of cold bacon, a tin of marmalade, and a loaf of bread there were the materials for a good breakfast for the five of us—Goyle, Evans, myself, and the other two platoon commanders.

Our dream of lolling round the sugar refinery all day in reserve was early dispelled. We had barely finished breakfast when the order came that we were to pack up and march off. We went back the way we had come towards the line we had been holding overnight.

As we were marching along the rumour spread that we were going back in support of the Westshires, and that there was an attack impending. We halted in some dead ground, and lined a ditch four or five hundred yards behind the line the Westshires were holding. As we were lying there an orderly came up with a message which Goyle was to read and pass on. Goyle showed me the bit of paper before folding it up again. The message ran:

The —th Brigade will attack at 10 a.m. in support of the French attack on —— on their right.

It was then nine o'clock, so we had an hour to wait. Goyle was much excited by the message, and said we were certain to be sent up to swell the Westshires' line. The men were still wearing the greatcoats they had had on during the night, and he ordered them to be taken off and put away in the packs. He also advised the platoon commanders to take off their mackintoshes, which show up an officer clearly.

While these preparations were going on I took a stroll down the ditch to battalion headquarters, hoping to find somewhere to leave my greatcoat instead of having to carry it. Battalion headquarters were behind a small house at the junction of a cross-roads. Here other people had collected—the stout officer, the doctor, and an artillery observing officer. The artillery observing officer was in telephonic communication with a heavy battery about two miles back, to which he was sending back messages about possible targets and the effect of fire. Outside the scout officer was making an early lunch off a piece of ham which he had found in the mess-box. I joined him, contributing a biscuit.

"The major is an ass, you know," he said; "he will go showing himself."

He pointed to our senior major, a very gallant officer indeed, but a man who had, as the scout officer said, an unfortunate tendency to expose himself to fire. He was at the moment standing at the cross-roads, beyond the shelter of the cottage, looking through his field-glasses in the direction of the enemy's lines. The cross-roads at which he was standing was a most exposed place. The major was a smart, dapper-looking man, and he stood with his legs apart, one hand holding the glasses, the other brushing his moustache. Suddenly there was a sharp *ping*; he dropped the glasses, raised his right foot sharply, and swore. Then he came limping in.

"Curse the brutes—curse the brutes," he said, sitting on the ground and nursing his foot; "they have shot me through the big toe."

The doctor went to the major's assistance and the scout officer peered round the corner of the house to see if he could make out where the shot had come from. Presently he came back.

I think they have got a Maxim up in that church tower, sir," he said.

There was a fine church in the town the enemy were holding, and the tower stood high up above the other buildings.

"Have they, by Gad—the brutes," said the major, still nursing his injured foot, which was causing him acute pain. "Here, let me look" he limped to the corner. A Maxim could plainly be heard firing from somewhere in front, *ping-ping-ping—ping-ping-ping.*

"By Jove, I believe you are right," said the major. "Here, just send that gunnery officer to me."

The artillery observing subaltern came up.

"Look here, they've got a Maxim in that church tower—see, over there—thing hit me in the foot just now. Can you telephone back and get your guns to it?"

"Yes, sir," said the gunnery subaltern.

Soon four heavy guns were playing on the church tower, and the tower crumbled. So are churches and other things destroyed in war time.

It was now nearly ten, and we returned to our trench. Soon bullets came whistling overhead, and we knew the attack had been launched. We lay low in the dugouts waiting till we were wanted. Knowing the ground, I could picture clearly what was going on in front, and I did not envy the Westshires their task. I could imagine them getting out of their trenches and advancing in line over that murderous stretch of plough-land. When we had been in the trenches they were then leaving we had hardly dared show our noses above them; but now the Westshires had the order, and out they had to go, and forward. *Phzz-phzz-phzz.* The bullets began to come over more quickly, and we could hear the answering fire of the Westshires. It may have been half an hour that we lay there, and then a hot, dusty figure crawled round the corner of the trench.

"Is the Captain of B Company there?"

"Yes, I'm here," Goyle answered.

The new arrival squatted down in the trench. It was the adjutant of the Westshires. He pulled out his pouch and started to fill his pipe. His hands shook so that he could hardly get the tobacco into the bowl. I shall never forget the way he breathed—hard, noisy gasps. The man was evidently at breaking-point.

"How is it going?" Goyle asked.

"Oh, it's hell," the adjutant of the Westshires answered.

"It is impossible to expect men to advance over such ground. We have only got about twenty yards. We have had a hundred down already—Leary and Blake are gone—Jones and Barty wounded. It is no good—they can't carry on. Look here; what I came back for was, would you send an officer with me, so that I can show him where we want your men? Our fellows are rather shaken. I think it would be a good thing if they would close up behind. One never knows what might happen."

I could read the adjutant's thoughts. He dreaded lest his men should break. He knew if they had to advance farther they would be shot down like rabbits. Poor man, he as adjutant of the regiment was responsible for the men's lives and conduct. The regiment was in danger of being wiped out. No wonder his hand shook, and he breathed in great gasps. Never have I seen a man so cruelly strained. He grew calmer as he sat there, and presently Goyle sent me back with him.

The adjutant of the Westshires was quite calm as we returned to the firing-line. We found the colonel of the regiment sitting on the ground behind a wall. He held a message in his hands. "Look there!" He read out the message to the adjutant:

The —th Brigade will continue their attack on at 11.30 a.m. The attack will be pressed home at all costs.

Both men looked at each other. They knew they had received the regiment's death warrant.

No attack could succeed over such ground.

The colonel looked at his watch. I looked at the little iron-grey man sitting there waiting for the hour when he was to send his regiment to their doom. Then the adjutant took me quietly, and showed me the places where he wished our men to come up. He was quite calm now as we peeped round the corner of a house at the lines which had to be taken at all costs. The firing had stopped now. The Westshires were lying out in the plough-land at the point they had reached. The Germans lined their trenches waiting for them to move. But the time never came. Ten minutes later a staff officer had come up, inspected the ground, and cancelled the second order for the attack.

19

By the Skin of Our Teeth

We were moved to the village very suddenly. There was no reason that we could see for the move. However, this transpired later. It was getting dusk when we reached the village. A and C Companies were sent at once up to the firing line, and B and D Companies were lined along a ditch in support. The ditch had been prepared for habitation by the regiment who had held it before. At one point they had thrown some boards across the ditch and made a house underneath. This proved a very welcome shelter when later it came on to rain. We lay in the ditch for an hour or two listening to the last shells before nightfall, from one of our heavy batteries, singing overhead.

The shells were sent in groups of three, and we could plainly hear each, *whizz-whizz-whizz*, chasing each other through the air, perhaps not more than twenty yards apart. We were comfortable enough where we were, and idly speculated on what errand of destruction the shells were bent. They sounded nasty great things to have coming in the wrong direction, and we wished the Germans joy of them.

About eight I felt hungry, and got out of the trench to have a look round. I had two tins of Mc'Conochie in my haversack, which I put in a pan of boiling water. Across a field to the front I saw a farm, and decided to go over and explore. In the field there were two or three curious heaps of straw, which proved to be the burial piles of dead cows, killed by shell fire, and covered over by the farmer in this rather ineffective fashion. The cows were getting smelly, and I did not stay long looking at them. I found the farm occupied by two old men and an old woman. One of the old men, over eighty, they told me, had taken to his bed and lain there with the shutters up for three days. He was half-dead from fright and could not be induced to move.

The old woman said they had had Germans billeted in the farm a week before. They had treated her and her old husband none too gently, driving them out of the house while they made soup in her cauldron. She had managed to hide one or two little bits of bread, and was making supper off a crust and some coffee She put the fire at my disposal for getting supper ready for Goyle and the other officer in the company. They all came across a quarter of an hour later, Evans with a great possession—a tin of cocoa. There was plenty of milk to be had from the farm—indeed, it was a godsend to the old people to get a man to milk their cows—and we soon had a beautiful jug of thick, steaming cocoa. We then prepared the Mc'Conochie, and what proved to be our last meal all together was a good one.

It was getting late when we had finished, and we had to hurry back to the support trench. On the way, as I was going along at a quick trot, I came head over heels over a big object and nearly impaled myself on a spike. Apart from the smell of the cow, it was really most dangerous lying out there at night-time and I sent a party of men back to bury it.

The trenches we were to take over lay just beyond the village along the crest of a slope. The section my company was responsible for ran just in front of three haystacks. A company extended away to our right, and the Dorchester Regiment continued the line to our left. The officer of the regiment we were relieving said to me: "You see those stacks—well, I should keep clear of them; the enemy have them set." I nodded, very tired at finding myself back in the firing-line, where we had been almost continuously for ten days, and not particularly interested in what the enemy had set or what they had not. In fact, as soon as I had seen the men distributed along the trench, and had given one or two orders about its improvement, I made straight for the centre stack, pulled as much hay as I could out of the side of it, rolled myself up, and went to sleep.

I was awakened by a sharp blow in the back. Looking up I saw Evans drawing his foot back to give me a second and harder kick.

"Get up, you blithering fool," he said; "your men are out all over the place."

I jumped to my feet, and, fastening my belt as I ran, dashed for the trench. I owed a lot to Evans for waking me. As Evans said, the men were all walking about outside the trench. I got them in immediately, and was preparing to follow when I thought of my bed, and went off to fetch it. One never knew when the next chance of leaving the trench might come I was bending down, gathering a good armful of hay, when there was a report, a sensation like red-hot iron running through one, followed by acute pain, and I pitched head-forward into the hay. I had been hit. Very frightened and hurt, I crawled as fast as I could round to the side farthest from the enemy and sat down. I examined my wounds—a bullet through each leg.

The shots were low down and did not look very serious. They hurt infernally, and I made a mental note to call the next man who said he never noticed he had been hit in the heat of an action a liar. I examined the wounds. Were they serious enough to warrant a visit to the field-dressing station and a possible return to England? I hoped devoutly they were. An attempt to stand soon satisfied me, and I fell down again, much relieved. All these thoughts were a matter of seconds; in the meanwhile there was a good deal going on round the stack. An enemy battery was playing round it with high-explosive shrapnel. The shells burst first one side, then the other, in front, behind, in all directions. The noise was deafening, and the lead in the air was just like a hailstorm; however, it was a stout stack, and kept me dry, though I confess I doubted getting away alive.

After a few minutes the firing stopped, and, throwing myself on my side, I rolled as fast as I could for a support trench. I pitched head-first into the trench and landed on the top of two privates who were sheltering in the bottom expecting more shrapnel over at any minute. They were not expecting me, and thought their last hour had come when I fell on top of them. Getting our breath, we all three cursed each other. Then, seeing I was an officer, they became respectful. I explained I was wounded, and they helped me off with my *puttees* and bound up the wounds with the first-aid bandage which I ripped from my coat. In the meanwhile word was sent back for stretcher-bearers.

As the firing had stopped these came up immediately, lifted me out of the trench, put me on a stretcher, and started off with me. We had to go down a road in full view of the enemy. For some providential reason they never fired at us, though I was about the last wounded man to be brought down that road. Halfway down the road the stretcher-bearers began to show signs of feeling my weight. I coaxed them on a few more yards, but when they came to the lee of cottage they put me down and shook their heads; another bearer came to the rescue, and with the extra help the party proceeded. A hundred yards more brought us to a cottage which was being used as a field-dressing station. The cottage was beginning to fill and wounded men lay about all over the floor.

"Oh, Gawd! Oh—!—ooh!!"

"Shut up, can't yer?" a man shouted from the far corner of the room.

"I've got a 'ole in me big enough to put yer 'and in," the sufferer explained, and began again to groan and swear.

"Got a cigarette, mate?" A man deathly pale on a stretcher held out his hand to a comrade who was slightly wounded and standing beside him. The latter extricated a Woodbine from a crumpled packet and passed it down. The man on the stretcher lit the cigarette and puffed at it phlegmatically. It was doubtful whether he would live, and though he did not know this, he knew he must not have anything to eat or drink for many hours.

About fifteen or twenty of us were lying on the floor of a cottage. Outside, four or five hundred yards up the street, a lively fight was in progress for the possession of the village. After the firing-line the cottage seemed a haven of peace and safety.

"Hullo, they've got you."

"Morning, Doctor."

A young fellow, fresh from his training at a hospital, was standing beside me. He was our regimental doctor, and I'd always thought of him as a lucky fellow who rode on a horse when we were on the march, got his rations regularly at all times, and during a scrap enjoyed the security of the extra few hundred yards which he was supposed to have between his dressing-station and the firing-line. Well, here he was to look after me, anyhow.

"Got a bit of work to do today, Doctor," I said as he bound me up.

"Yes," he answered, adjusting a blanket as a pad under me, "there, just keep in that position and the bleeding will soon stop." He turned to the man next me.

"I've got some across the way, too," he said, as the orderly handed him fresh bandages. "They've been shelling the poor beggars, knocking all the slates off the roof."

As he spoke some shrapnel crashed against the roof of our cottage, sending a few tiles rattling to the ground. The doctor looked up.

"I think we're all right here," he said. "We've got a double roof. I always try to pick a cottage with a double roof. But those poor devils over the way are getting awful scared; I think I'll slip across to them."

The bit of road he had to "slip across" was catching most of the shells which the cottage did not, and was also the channel for a steady stream of rifle and machine-gun fire. I began to see there wasn't much in it, whether one was a doctor or a platoon commander.

More especially did I realise a doctor's difficulties when, later in the day, just as our doctor had finished looking at my dressings, a message came that the field-dressing station belonging to the regiment on our left had been set alight by a shell. He hastily organised a party of stretcher-bearers and orderlies and went off at once. Later he came back. He said it had been terrible to see the wounded lying helpless in the barn waiting for the flames, but somehow they had managed to rescue all and move them to a safer place, though the whole operation had to be carried out under rifle and shell fire. Each time a regiment is seriously engaged with the enemy at least 100 men are hit, often four times the number. The regimental doctor is supposed to bind up each one of these, and often when times are slack and a stray man here or there gets hit he will be sent for to come up to the trenches.

"'Allo, Jock," loud greetings were shouted by every one in the room to a little man standing in the doorway with a *bandolier* across his chest and rifle with bayonet still fixed. He was a grubby little fellow, with blood and mud caked all down his cheek, ragged clothes, and— as I had seen as he came up the cottage steps—A pronounced limp. It was Private Mutton, scallywag, humorist, and well-known character in the regiment.

"Yus, they got me," he said in answer to inquiries, "fro' me calf," he pointed to his leg, "and right acrost the top of me 'ead"—he raised his cap and showed where a bullet had parted his hair, grazing the scalp. "But I give the bloke somethink what did it." Private Mutton grinned at his bayonet. "Got 'im fair, right fro' 'is stomick."

I could not help feeling delighted, for I recognised in the muddy, gory, highly-pleased-with-himself little man the original of Thomas Atkins, of whose doings along the Indian frontier I had read thrilling accounts by Mr. Kipling, and whose quaint mannerisms I had often laughed at as represented on the stage of music-halls at home. . . .

At 9 p.m. the ambulances came up.

The doctor went round quickly attending to each man. He bound up my wounds afresh and had me carried into an inner room I lay there all day, and never shall I forget the experience. I could see nothing except a bit of the wall on the opposite side of the street. But I could hear. Just after I had been brought in fresh firing broke out. Rifle fire this rime, sharp and insistent. Then there was a sound of stamping feet, and I heard an officer rallying the men at the corner of the street. The firing continued all day and sometimes seemed to age almost at the door of the cottage.

I gathered that the Germans were attacking the village in masses, and that it was touch-and-go whether we could hold out. Sometimes there would be a rush of men outside the window, and I would look to see if the pale grey uniform was there or if khaki still held the place. Every now and then a shower of shrapnel struck the roof of the cottage, and tiles went rattling to the road. All the while a section of our artillery fired incessantly. How gallant those guns of ours sound— *Boom-boom-boom*. They were fighting to their last shell. If the village went, they went with it. No horses could be brought up to draw them away in such an inferno.

The doctor worked on quietly. His work extended now to houses on the left and right. He said it was terrible to see the fear of death on the faces of men shot through the stomach. He found time once to have a cup of tea with me and smoke a cigarette. Night began to fall and the room grew dark. I was glad of his company for five minutes. We were in the same boat, he told me—if the Germans got the village he was going to stay behind with the wounded.

At half-past five Evans came in with a smashed arm.

"Goyle has gone," he said. "He was hit twice before during the day. He was holding out with a few men there and got a third through the chest which did him. Edwards was shot through the knee, and we had to leave him. All the company officers are down. A company has been surrounded and cut off. Whew! you can't live out there." As he spoke the firing swelled to a din unequalled through the day. We heard shouts and curses. The Germans were making a final tremendous effort to break through.

"Our boys may do it," said Evans, "but there are not many left." I lay back against the wall, pulled out a cigarette, and threw one to Evans. We could only wait. Suddenly outside we heard a stamp of feet, a hoarsely yelled order, "Fix bayonets!" another word of command, and a mass of men rushed past the window up the street, cheering madly. "That's the ——s," cried a stretcher-bearer, who came in excitedly. "They have been sent up from the reserve."

The doctor came in. "We've got two more regiments up; we shall be all right now," he said.

For a moment the firing continued, then died down. Night came and found us still holding the village, and at ten o'clock the ambulance took us away.

20

"And Thence to Bed"

The horse ambulance took us back some three miles to the field ambulance, where we spent the night after being given some food and tea and having our wounds dressed. The accommodation was rough, just some straw on the floor, but to feel there were three miles between ourselves and the enemy gave one quite a feeling of being rested. At these field ambulances the work of dressing the wounded goes on incessantly day and night, and it is here that many a case of lockjaw or gangrene is prevented by the timely application of anti-tetanus injection or iodine. Among the wounded was a young German boy, not more than eighteen years old. The other wounded Tommies and the orderlies were very good to him, making quite a pet of the boy and giving him tea and cigarettes and asking him what he thought about the war. He had only had six weeks' training before being sent into the firing-line, and was a gentle enough creature bewildered by the fierce struggle into which he had been thrown.

In the morning a fleet of motor ambulances came to take us to the clearing hospital at railhead. Most of these ambulances were private cars fitted up at their owners' expense and driven in many cases by the owners too. Only those who have been wounded and travelled in a Government horse ambulance can appreciate the good work done by these volunteer Red Cross workers and their cars. After the lumbering horse vehicle rubber tyres and the well-hung body of a private car are an unspeakable relief to broken bones. Our driver was a young fellow who looked as though he had just left Oxford or Cambridge. He drove us very slowly and carefully over the twelve miles of bumpy road, and took us straight to the station in time to have us put on a hospital train which was leaving that morning for the base.

How often at the beginning of the war on my way up to the

Front had I seen these hospital trains go by and wondered—with a very pious hope that it might be so—if it would ever be my lot to take a passage in one. In those days as now everyone knew that it was only a question of time before they were killed or wounded—few last long enough to become diseased—and to be stowed safely away in a hospital train labelled for England was the best fate that could befall anyone.

It was, then, with a feeling of supreme contentment that I allowed myself to be laid along the seat of a first-class carriage and propped up behind with a greatcoat and a pillow. On the opposite seat was a young gentleman not nearly so contented. He had been hit in the shoulder. He said his wound was hurting him; that he was not comfortable on the seat of the carriage; and that he considered tinned stew (which had just been brought us) a very nasty luncheon. I thought him a peevish and graceless cub and, when he snapped at the orderly who came to clear away lunch, rebuked him.

I said that he ought to be thankful for being where he was at all; that his wound was nothing compared to those of others in the train; that his whining and peevishness brought discredit on his uniform and regiment; and that he ought to be ashamed of himself for making such a fuss. As he was a second lieutenant just fresh from Sandhurst and I was an elderly subaltern of several years' service he did not argue with me, but looked at the floor, while I scowled at him from time to time across the carriage.

Eventually the train started and we began our journey to Boulogne. We had been told it would take about nine hours, and so prepared to make ourselves as comfortable as possible and sleep. Except for a visit from the doctor to ask if we wanted anything, and from a hospital nurse, nothing much happened for the rest of the day. The visit from the hospital nurse is one of the things I remember most clearly from an otherwise clouded period. It was the first taste of the infinite sympathy and solicitude which women give to men returned from the war. All who have experienced it—as every wounded man has in abundant measure —must have felt that anything he has suffered was worth such a reward.

After the visit from the hospital nurse we had some dinner and settled down for the night. About this time I began to notice that the blanket which had been folded in four and placed under my injured leg was slightly rucked at the corner. I could not reach it to adjust it myself and after the scene with my stable mate did not like to ask his assistance. Presently an orderly came by and I called him in to put it right. Half an hour later the same thing happened again and I had to call in another orderly. The little subaltern, who was dozing opened one eye and looked at me reproachfully, but said nothing.

Later, when the train pulled up with a jerk which nearly threw us off our seats, we both groaned softly, and when it did the same thing again I swore, and received a grateful look from the rebuked grumbler. In fact, to shorten the story, by noon the next day, when we were finally taken out of the train, I was half hysterical with pain, discomfort, and fatigue, and the little subaltern had nearly forgotten his troubles in his efforts to adjust my blankets with his sound arm and running to and fro fetching the orderly: the moral of this story needs no pointing. . . .

At Boulogne we were taken by motor ambulance to one of the base hospitals. The hospital was a marvellous example of efficient emergency organisation. Three days before it had been a hotel; and in this space of time—*i.e.* three days—the entire building had been converted into a thoroughly modern hospital with wards and operating-theatre. Most of the work had been done by the members of the hospital staff themselves, and, as we were taken in, the last bits of hotel furniture were still standing in the hall waiting to be removed.

By this time I was rather exhausted, and I cannot remember more than a matron in a dark silk dress with a very gentle, pretty face bending over me and asking me if I was comfortable, and my replying in a voice that was little above a whisper that it was good to be in bed. I think she said, too, something to the nurse about "not putting him to bed like that." I had been in the same clothes for a fortnight and they were very muddy, and I remember having my breeches cut off and being helped into a flannel night-shirt. I woke later to find a nurse beside me with a basin of water. "Would you like to wash?" she asked. I gazed at her apathetically. "Come on then, I'll do it for you," she said kindly. She dipped a piece of flannel in the basin and rubbed it gently over my face. Then she took one of my hands and rubbed that; then streaks of white appeared down my fingers as the caked mud was cleared. "There, I think that it all we'll do for the present," she said, and feeling beautifully clean—though in reality with ten days' beard and looking perfectly filthy—I lay back on the pillow.

After tea I sat up, accepted a cigarette from my neighbour, and took stock of the rest of the ward.

In the bed on my right was a man with a bandaged head; he had an orderly beside him and was dictating a letter. He was evidently feeling very weak, for he spoke with an obvious effort. The letter was about some lost baggage, and dictated with the utmost precision and detail. He ended by saying, "Signed James Brown, Captain and Adjutant;" and I couldn't help smiling, for it was so like an adjutant to dictate a precise letter about some lost baggage, but it seemed so funny for him, weakened by his wounds as he was, to be lying there in bed doing it, and I felt sure it was more from force of habit than anything else.

At eight o'clock the day-sister made a round of the wards with the night-sister, handing over her patients till the next day. The night-sister was followed by a sort of understudy who, I remember, was tall and thin with rather a long nose. This understudy, who was referred to as "nurse" by the other two, was, I gathered, a sort of probationer, and not allowed to take much responsibility on herself.

By ten the ward was in darkness except for one green-shaded light, and I think I must have dozed a little, for I remember looking up suddenly to see the night-sister's understudy standing at the foot of my bed and gazing at me with a puzzled expression. Seeing me open my eyes she stretched out her arm and pulled towards her a glass-topped table with a bowl of dressings on it. Then she studied me again. I was still half asleep and watched her with half-closed eyes.

"Is it your *feet?*" she asked.

I nodded.

She lifted the bedclothes back from the foot of the bed and surveyed my bandaged feet for a minute or two. Then with a sudden air of determination she bent down and, catching my right foot by the big toe, lifted it deftly off the pillow on which it was resting. I gave one piercing scream which woke the whole ward and brought the night-sister running in. For the rest of the night I lay with one eye peeping over the sheet prepared to yell for help at the top of my voice if the young lady assistant came near my bed. The next day she returned to England for further instruction.

The following afternoon I was operated on and the bullet extracted from my ankle. A sergeant brought it me wrapped in cotton-wool and left me feeling quite reassured about the success of the operation.

I remember very well on the way up to the Front seeing a hospital ship leave one of the base ports. She was a beautiful looking vessel, painted white, with a great red cross painted on either side amidships. That hospital ship certainly looked comfortable, and I don't mind admitting that, at the time, I wished most heartily I was on board her with my job done instead of having to go up to the firing-line and do it. The wounded men on board all looked so happy and comfortable.

However, everything comes to him who waits —nothing more quickly than a bullet in these sanguinary days—and after a week at the base hospital at Boulogne I was given a ticket marked "cot case" and told I was going to be put on board a hospital ship for England. I smiled gratefully at the doctor, tied the ticket round my neck, put on a woollen waistcoat, muffler, and dressing-gown (all presented to me by the hospital) over my pyjamas, and waited my turn to be carried downstairs. In due course, with three others, I was taken in a motor ambulance to the ship, and from thenceforward was in the charge of the naval authorities.

We were carried up the gangway on our stretchers and placed on a sort of luggage lift which in the twinkling of an eye transported us below, where we were lifted on to swinging cots arranged in a large saloon. The quick, handy way in which everything was done was typical of the navy, and having once spent six weeks on board a battleship, I felt quite at home again. Dinner was brought round soon after getting on board, and I ate soup, fish, roast mutton, and apple tart with the heartiest of appetites. Unfortunately, also, in the happiness of the moment, I drank a large bottle of Bass which seriously affected my slumbers during the night.

We did not leave until the following night, arriving at Plymouth at nine o'clock the next morning. However, it was no hardship to be aboard the hospital ship.

The cots were just as comfortable as beds; there was every appliance for dressing our wounds, and the nurses and doctors looked after us indefatigably. In such surroundings aspects of the war which are taken more seriously elsewhere are made light of. The patients made jokes about each other's wounds and their own, and all were so glad to be alive that pain and suffering were almost forgotten. There the middle of a silence suddenly uttered an exclamation of annoyance. Asked what was the matter, he said he wanted to know the time and had just discovered he had lost his watch. It was a wrist watch, he explained, and must have been left on the arm they had amputated at the field ambulance.

At Plymouth we were taken on board a launch and landed at a quay close by the naval hospital. The ingenious cots devised by the navy enable a wounded man to be moved bodily in his bed, all wrapped up and warm, to the bed in the hospital. They are so made that they can either be carried as stretchers, or slung from a ship's side, or put on hand-trolleys and wheeled. The Naval Hospital at Plymouth is a model of neatness and smartness, each patient in the officers' quarters gets a small room to himself which is called a cabin; the orderlies are all ex-sailors and handy and obliging as only sailors can be; and the naval nurses in their smart blue uniforms are a pleasure to watch.

I stayed at Plymouth for five days, when I was allowed to travel to London.

www.ingramcontent.com/pod-product-compliance
Lightning Source LLC
Chambersburg PA
CBHW032050080426
42733CB00006B/228